The
Alvin
Karpis
Story

The Alvin Karpis Story

by Alvin Karpis

with Bill Trent

COWARD, McCANN & GEOGHEGAN, INC.

NEW YORK

Library of Congress Catalog Card Number: 78-136446
PRINTED IN THE UNITED STATES OF AMERICA

CONTENTS

INTRODUCTION

The autobiography of Alvin Karpis is not a nice book. It is, in fact, an icy, brutal one. But it is a truthful book that stands on its own as an inside look at what crime is and who criminals really are. There is no attempt to pretty up the picture.

Crime is an icy, brutal business.

Too often, however, books about crime and criminals are written by professional writers or social workers who try to explain what it is all about. Seldom, except in a book like this, does the reader get the real story, because few criminals have the chance to set it down in their own words— usually there is somebody working with them, evading something here, explaining away something there.

7

Alvin Karpis makes no excuses for what he was. Today he has no regrets. His attitude is, I think, best expressed in something I read in the first issue of *Scanlan's* magazine. Before he died, Ben Hecht was working on a biography of Mickey Cohen. After Hecht's death, *Scanlan's* published the manuscript, or the part of it that had been completed. In this fragment, Hecht wrote:

I have been talking to Mickey Cohen for a number of years and mingling with his underworld entourage. Out of my contacts has come what I think may be a major piece of anthropological lore. The criminal has no hates or fears—except very personal ones. He is possibly the only human left in the world who looks lovingly on society. He does not hanker to fight it, reform it or even rationalize it. He wants only to rob it. He admires it as a hungry man might admire a roast pig with an apple in its mouth.

I was pleased to find this out, for I have read much to the contrary. Society does not, as sociologists and other tony intellectuals maintain, create the criminal. Bad housing, bad companions, bad government, etc., have little to do with why there are killers, robbers and outlaws. The criminal has no relation to society to speak of. He is part of man's soul, not his institutions. He is an old one. A thousand preachers, summer boy's camps, plus a congress of psychiatrists can barely dent even a minor criminal. As for the major criminal, he cannot be touched at all by society because he operates on a different time level. He is the presocial part of us—the ape that spurned the collar. . . .

The criminal at the time of his lawlessness is one of the few happy or contented men to be found among us. . . .

While he remains a criminal he is as free of conscience pangs as the most right-doing of bookkeepers. He eats well, sleeps well, lives well, and his only disadvantage is that he may die ahead of his time from an enemy bullet, the gas chamber or electric chair.

So lived Mickey Cohen and so lived Alvin Karpis. Creatures of a slightly different environment, perhaps, but both alike.

Karpis knew he was going to be a criminal from the time he was ten and stole his first gun. In his teens, when he was already one of the most feared and/or respected (depending on which side of the law you may have been) guns in the Midwest, he was a criminal. A very cold and efficient criminal. Within a single decade he became a legend. There were bank robberies and shoot-outs. There were kidnappings and train holdups. He became top gun with the infamous Karpis-Ma Barker Gang, which is now part of North America's underworld mythology. At one time he was wanted for nearly a score of murders in fourteen different states.

Ma and Freddie Barker died in a hail of FBI machine-gun bullets, but Karpis, nicknamed Old Creepy by the police, survived to become Public Enemy Number One.

Mind you, it never occurred to me that someday I would meet Alvin Karpis. In fact, as a wide-eyed kid who followed the exploits of the gun-slinging desperadoes in the 1930's— the Dillingers, the Pretty Boy Floyds, the Baby Face Nelsons —in the newspapers, it never occurred to me that these people really existed. It made for exciting reading. But to me those characters were no more real than those upright, death-defying types I came across in the simon-pure *Boys' Own* annual.

Anyway, of all these outlaws the one who really captured my fancy was Alvin "Old Creepy" Karpis. At least it gave a kid more goose pimples than nicknames like Pretty Boy or Baby Face or Legs.

Old Creepy was a nickname to have nightmares by.

Or perhaps, as all this death and violence was more of a game to me than a brutal reality, it was a kid's normal desire to go with a winner. Because, in his own lawless world, Karpis was a winner. Once the Associated Press ran a kind of box score for hoodlums, listing such luminaries as Clyde Barrow and Bonnie Parker, Dillinger, Ma Barker, Nelson, and Floyd.

But the name at the top of the list was Karpis.

Frankly, I thought I had forgotten all of this until about seven years ago when I heard that Karpis was still alive. So I got in touch with him in jail and kept in touch. This was not done out of any feeling of admiration—in fact, quite the reverse. But I was curious. And also I felt that Karpis might have a worthwhile story to tell. Not a prettied-up version like the Bonnie and Clyde movie effort which turned murder and sadism into something kind of appealing. What I wanted was a realistic "I was there" account of what it was like to be both the hunter and the hunted and what would make a man deliberately choose a gun as an everyday working tool.

When he was paroled and deported to his native Canada, Karpis agreed to provide this for me. That was almost two years ago. Bill Trent, a staff writer with *Weekend Magazine,* was attached to Karpis, and together they went to work.

It was a much longer, but better, project than I had expected. Karpis has almost total recall. Names, places, dates—they all came pouring out. Finally we had 600,000 words on tape. Trent, of course, then had to check these cold, unvarnished facts of robbery, kidnapping, and mayhem. Then he had to hone all those words and all that research down to a book-size package.

There are things in this book that may disgust you. There are other incidents that may make you laugh, because even violence has its freakish moments. And there are accounts which you may question—because they smash some long-established legends.

J. Edgar Hoover, for instance, told the world he had personally captured Karpis. This was at a time in 1936 when Hoover's personal courage was under attack in Congress and his fledgling FBI operation in danger. After the Karpis incident was publicized, nobody dared criticize Hoover or his organization.

As Karpis says: "I made that son of a bitch."

There is also Karpis' account of his long association with Ma Barker and her sons. There has been a book written about Ma Barker and a movie, called *Bloody Mama*. The official history of the FBI also gives her a lot of attention. The Karpis account is shockingly different.

These are just two of the items which will make this book the subject of intense controversy for some time to come and a must for those interested in the true story of the growth of crime in North America.

Can the word of an admitted thief be trusted—can it stack up, for instance, against the official history of the FBI? There is no final answer to this. But Bill Trent never once, in all his checking, found a Karpis story to be in error. Also, as kind of supervising editor of the project, I spent a lot of time with Karpis in the last two years. Today Karpis is soft-spoken, always immaculately dressed. He lives quietly, but enjoys the good things of life. When we lunch together he prefers two of Montreal's more elegant eating places—the Beaver Club in the Queen Elizabeth Hotel and the Maritime Bar in the Ritz Carlton Hotel. If he is entertaining lady friends, his sister, who now lives in Chicago, or the young woman he intends to marry, he likes to reserve a corner table in Altitude 737, a restaurant atop Montreal's Place Ville Marie with a breathtaking view of the city.

But Karpis is still a man with a strong will and a fierce pride. He will talk easily and naturally about his days and years of crime and the long years he spent in Alcatraz— more time on the island than any other man—and in the federal penitentiary on McNeil Island. Don't try to lump Karpis with "the Mob," though, or refer to him as an ordinary hoodlum, as Hoover did after his prize catch.

"I'm no hoodlum," Karpis snapped. "And I don't like to be called a hood. I'm a thief."

"As far as I'm concerned, you're a hoodlum," Hoover replied.

Karpis tried to explain the difference: "A thief," he said, "is anybody who gets out and works for his living, like robbing a bank, or breaking into a place and stealing stuff, or kidnapping somebody. He really gives some effort to it. A hoodlum is a pretty lousy kind of scum. He works for gangsters and bumps off guys after they've been put on the spot. Why, after I'd made my rep, some of the Chicago Syndicate wanted me to go to work for them as a hood—you know, handling a machine gun. They offered me two hundred and fifty dollars a week and all the protection I needed. I was on the lam at the time and not able to work at my regular line. But I wouldn't consider it. 'I'm a thief,' I said, 'I'm no lousy hoodlum.' "

Hoover merely replied, "From my standpoint, you're still a hoodlum."

As Lew Louderback, in his book *The Bad Ones*, observed: "It was a rather shabby way to treat the man who had just contributed the final touches to the FBI's most glorious legend."

Anyway, this is the Karpis story, as taped and verified by Bill Trent. I really do not know what anybody will think of it—all three of us have been living with it too long now to pass accurate judgment on it. But I do know one thing. After reading it, I don't think any kid will be tempted to take up the calling of professional gunman.

Montreal, August 9, 1970   FRANK LOWE

1

"My Profession Was Robbing Banks"

MY PROFESSION WAS robbing banks, knocking off payrolls, and kidnapping rich men. I was good at it. Maybe the best in North America for five years, from 1931 to 1936. I'm not trying to boost my ego when I use a fancy word like profession to describe the way I earned my living. My work became a profession because that's how I approached it. In another set of circumstances, I might have turned out to be a top lawyer or maybe a big-time businessman. I might have made it to any high position that demanded brains and style and a cool, hard way of handling yourself. Certainly I could have held the highest job there was in any line of police detection work. I outthought, outwitted, and just plain defeated enough cops and G-men in my time to recognize that I was more knowledgeable about crime than any of them, including the number-one guy, J. Edgar Hoover of the Federal Bureau of Investigation. But the way life worked out for me, the way the breaks went especially when I was a kid, I didn't turn out to be a lawyer, a businessman, or a G-man. I became a robber, a heister, and a kidnapper. And I was a pro.

I don't know how much money I made. I lost count. I'm a guy with total recall and can recite details of almost every bank stickup, every heist, every crime I pulled in the years that Freddie Barker and I and all the other members of the Karpis-Barker Gang were running wild through the American Midwest. But it's impossible even for me to figure out how much cash I took in. All I know is that in the good days, we all lived pretty high. We always had money to buy the best food, live in the hotels and apartments we liked, wear good clothes, and drive big, fast cars.

The trouble was that I had to be pretty cagey about spending my money. I was a fugitive all my adult life, and I had to keep my eye out for the cops every second of the day and night. I may have had plenty of cash, but I couldn't go around making waves like a normal, well-to-do businessman. I didn't exactly hang out in high society. Instead, when I was looking for a good time, I'd head with Freddie and the others to a speakeasy or a whorehouse. The people in those places were great. I could relax there. We all had the same thing in common—plenty of money and the cops waiting to take it away from us.

I got into crime to earn that money and I stayed in it to keep on turning a big dollar. But I wasn't entirely what you'd call mercenary about my profession. I got a kick out of it apart from the money. The action and excitement thrilled me. I enjoyed the challenge of planning a job and carrying out each step with military precision. Our jobs weren't haphazard operations. At least not after we broke into the big time. We were professionals at our work, and we figured out timing, escape routes, each guy's individual job, and all the other details of every robbery or kidnapping as if we were laying out the strategy for a combat attack in a war.

For all the planning, though, a job could go wrong. And when I say "wrong," I'm not talking about a minor slipup. I mean that some stickups could turn into total disasters. I'm thinking of a classic mess we ran into when we set out to rob the bank in the little town of Concordia, Kansas. That happened in the spring of 1932 when I was twenty-four years old, and if any Hollywood studio had figured on making a movie out of the Concordia job, they couldn't have starred Edward G. Robinson or Jimmy Cagney in it. It would have been a natural for Buster Keaton or Laurel and Hardy.

There were five of us involved—me, Freddie Barker, Lawrence Devol, Jess Doyle, and Earl Christman. Christman was in on it because he needed money. He was a specialist in con games and swindles and he'd been doing time at Jackson, Michigan. He escaped when some sheriff's men from Seattle were escorting him to the Coast to testify in a trial of three train robbers. He was on the lam with no cash, and we took him into the Concordia job as a favor, even though he didn't have any holdup experience. There was a lot of cooperation like that among us. You learned to help your own kind because you never knew when you might need a favor yourself. Jess Doyle was like Christman— Concordia was his first stickup too. He was an experienced bank burglar who'd broken into more than his share of banks by night and cracked open their safes, but he'd never before walked through a front door with a loaded gun in his hand in broad daylight.

The other three of us were seasoned hands. Freddie Barker was one of my closest friends. He was a tough guy when he had to be, a robber who never hesitated to shoot his way out of trouble. On some occasions, he didn't mind starting the trouble either, particularly when a cop was in his way.

He was a son of the famous Ma Barker and, for years, Freddie, his brother Doc, Ma, and I lived together in different towns in the Midwest where I suppose, the legend of the Karpis-Barker Gang got started.

The other guy on the Concordia job, Lawrence Devol, had worked with me over several years. I first met him in 1926 in prison in Hutchinson, Kansas. I was serving a five-to-ten-year sentence for burglary, and I hadn't been in the place very long before I began to hit it off with this dark, mild-talking guy, about five or six years older than me, who seemed to know everything about beating safes. That was Devol and he was a great teacher. We broke out of Hutchinson together and in later years we hooked up for dozens of holdups.

The five of us were living with Ma Barker in a big house out at White Bear Lake, northeast of St. Paul, Minnesota, when we decided to take the Concordia bank. We didn't discuss the job while Ma was around. We never did. Contrary to the stories that were later spread in books and movies, ·Ma took no role in any crimes we pulled. In fact, all her life she was kept completely in the dark about our plans. Up at White Bear Lake, we followed the same practice we always followed. When we wanted to discuss a holdup, we hopped in one of our cars and took off. A car was the safest, most private spot anyone could imagine, free from any possibility of eavesdropping by the cops—or Ma.

The first step in the overall plan was to run the roads in the Concordia area. That was standard operating procedure on any job. What we did was run a car up and down and around every dirt road, back road, and gravel track until we knew the district like the backs of our hands. Then we plotted the route out of Concordia we figured would fool the police—that would take us down the least populated roads. Once we decided on a particular route, we put it down with absolute accuracy in a notebook. We started in front of the

Concordia bank with the odometer at zero and drove our course. Every time we turned off one road onto another, we wrote the mileage in the book. We did the same with every landmark—red barn on the right at so many miles, stone house on the left at another point. After driving the route several times, we had the escape course down pat.

Running the roads also meant hiding gasoline at strategic points. Our first plant was twenty-five miles from the bank. Gas caches were important since the cops had a nasty habit of shooting holes in our tanks as we drove away from the scenes of our crimes. We made a practice of carrying corks to plug the leaks, but we'd usually lose plenty of gas before we could stop the car to jam the plugs in. Under all those circumstances, a fresh tank of gas only twenty-five miles away made a lot of sense.

On the Concordia job, we figured on driving back to the St. Paul area, a distance of almost seven hundred miles. It took a lot of road running to work out a safe route over so many miles, especially when we had to avoid main highways and roads through large towns where cops might be laying for us. We planned carefully, laid out half a dozen gasoline drops and, for good measure, deposited a thermos of hot coffee and some sandwiches at one of them.

We cased the bank, located the vault and each employee's station, and assigned each of our guys to a specific job. It looked like a pushover and we allowed ourselves about seven or eight minutes to grab the money and hit the road for St. Paul. We put on overalls because they were the clothing that most men in the area wore. In this way we could blend in with the scenery.

Then, in the middle of the morning on a sunny day, we hit the bank. Doyle waited outside behind the wheel of the car. Christman stood just inside the bank door, holding some dollar bills in his hand as if he had just made a deposit. His job was to take charge of customers as they came in. With luck, he wouldn't have much to do because we'd be in and out of the place before many customers arrived.

Devol, Freddie, and I walked in and took a quick look around. There were seven or eight employees behind the counter, and the only customers in sight were two old farmers sitting on a bench eating their lunches out of brown paper bags. We pulled our guns and, speaking in low voices, told everyone to move quietly and quickly into the small back room. The staff people did what they were told, but the farmers just kept on chewing. We waved our guns at them and cleared the room. They still didn't move. Freddie, Devol, and I just stared at one another. Finally Devol stood over them with his gun.

"We're robbing this bank," he said. He spoke slowly, deliberately.

Well, Jesus, they hotfooted it then into the back room with the rest of the staff. The incident cost us only a small delay, but it was an omen of events to come.

The three of us cleaned out the cages in swift time and loaded the money into army barracks bags, which all professional bank robbers carried. Then Devol and Freddie took the head cashier into the vault and asked him to unlock the safe. It was one of the those big round cannonballs with a time lock. The lock wasn't on that day, but the cashier admitted he had the combination to open the thing.

"Open it," Devol ordered him.

"No," he said.

"Open the safe—fast," Devol shouted.

The cashier was a real stubborn Dutchman and he just shook his head.

I was watching Devol and Freddie and the cashier through the door, and when they started their dispute, I walked back into the main banking area to check on things. Through the window, I could see Doyle still sitting behind the wheel pretending to read a paper. Under it, he was holding a machine gun. Christman, meanwhile, was having his first taste of action. A couple of customers came in and he told them, just as we'd coached him, that there was a robbery and they should move into the back room. Christman handled himself smoothly.

I returned to the vault.

"Open this thing or I'll belt you," Devol was saying to the cashier.

"No."

Devol slapped the guy, but it did no good. He was a determined son of a bitch.

I went into the back room, picked out the nicest-looking girl, and led her into the vault. I poked the gun in her stomach. It was a forty-five automatic with a twenty-shot clip, a wicked-looking weapon that resembled a machine gun more than a pistol. The girl's eyes popped when she felt the muzzle of the forty-five.

"Open the safe," she pleaded with the cashier. "Please. Money is one thing. Our lives are another."

I could see she wasn't reaching this guy at all, so I broke in. "If you don't open up," I warned, "I'm going to blow this girl in two."

I had no intention of shooting. But by saying this, I thought it might help the cashier save face. I reasoned that he could open the safe and say afterward that he had to do it in order to save the girl's life.

He was awfully stubborn, though. He just looked at me and hardly blinked an eye. "You go ahead if you want to," he said. "She doesn't belong to me. If you want to shoot her, then shoot her. But I'm not going to open the safe."

I returned the girl to the back room. By now we'd been in the bank twenty minutes. Two more customers came in. Christman told them a robbery was on and steered them into the back room. Then a boy of about eleven or twelve walked in. I took him by the arm.

"Kid," I said, "we're robbing this bank. We don't want to hurt you."

"Get your lousy hands off me," he said.

More customers arrived and Christman just kept on directing them into the back room. I looked out the window and saw a waitress coming out of the restaurant across the street. She had a bankbook in her hand and some bills. Sure enough, she headed right through the front door of our bank.

"Hold it, miss," I said. "We're robbing this bank."

I took her to the back room. There they all stood, seven employees, the two deaf farmers, the twelve-year-old kid, and a dozen other customers. They were jammed up against each other. It was as crowded as a rush hour trolley in there.

"Well," I told the waitress, "I guess you'll have to sit under that table."

In the vault, the cashier was in trouble. Freddie and Devol had really slapped him, and he was bleeding from a big hole in his cheek. But he was sticking to his favorite word.

"Let's clean out the vault," Devol suggested. "Records and all." We did as he said.

"We can't stay here much longer," I said. It was already shaping up as one of the longest bank jobs in history.

Devol tried again with the cashier. "How would you like your eyes burned out?" he asked.

The Dutchman just shook his head.

I went back to Christman. "I put two more in the room," he said.

I looked out the window. Doyle was having his problems there too. A man and woman in the car behind ours had obviously seen what was going on in the bank, and Doyle had maneuvered our car to block them. They were sitting glued to their seats.

I checked up and down the street. There were no police. But across the street, in the restaurant, I could see a guy who seemed to be the owner handing another waitress a finger-waving lecture. She turned, pushed through the restaurant door, and crossed the street toward the bank.

"I suppose you're looking for your girlfriend," I said as soon as she stepped inside the door.

"Yeah," she said. "George is really sore. He thinks she's just fooling around."

"Well, we're robbing the bank," I said. I was getting awfully sick of that goddamn line. "Your friend is under the table in the back room and you'll have to crawl under there with her."

By this time, we'd been in the bank thirty-five minutes. The Concordia police still hadn't got wind of what was going on. Suddenly the bank door flew open and a man charged through. I turned my forty-five in his direction. It was the restaurant owner. He looked at the gun and his face froze.

"You son of a bitch," I yelled. I had to take my temper out on someone. "Your girls aren't fooling around. We're robbing this bank, and if there's any shooting, I'm starting with you."

I pushed him into the back room. It took a hefty shove, because by then the gang in there was crowded tight against the door.

"All right," Devol was saying to the cashier, "you got one more chance. Open up or I'll kill you."

He still said no.

"That's it, you guys," I said. "We've been in here for forty-five minutes. Let's go."

We left. The safe remained closed. The money was still inside. And the head cashier was sitting on the floor, mumbling through bleeding lips.

We took two girls with us as hostages. It was usual procedure in any job to make a couple of women ride outside on the running boards to discourage the cops from shooting at us. But there was no sign of the police in Concordia. They must have been even more incompetent that day than we were. Anyway, we let the girls off after a few miles and they thanked us.

We drove north from Concordia to leave the impression we were headed for Nebraska. Then we began zigzagging our way east. When we got stuck in the mud, we decided to back up and take a different road. The change in plans meant that our mileage maps weren't worth a damn, and we had to rely on regular road maps. If we intended to stick exclusively to main roads, they served the purpose. But for back roads, they were totally unreliable. Naturally we got lost.

By sheer luck we blundered our way out of Kansas and through Missouri. But in southern Minnesota we got screwed up in the dark and we tried to set a course for St. Paul on a compass we were carrying. The trouble was that all the guys had different ideas about how to read the compass. We finally gave that up and tried to trace our route by the stars.

"There's the Big Dipper," Doyle said, pointing to the sky. "As a night burglar I know what it looks like."

"You're crazy," Devol said. "I've been a night burglar too, and that's the Little Dipper you're pointing to."

The argument went on all night as we drove around in circles in the dark. It was hours before we made White Bear Lake, and we were fed up and exhausted. But one piece of news cheered us; we dumped the canvas bags from the bank on one of the beds and counted out $22,000 in cash.

Among the records we'd taken from the vault were some bonds as well, mostly nonnegotiable, and one other funny-looking document.

"Look at this," Devol said. "We've stolen the deed to the Concordia courthouse."

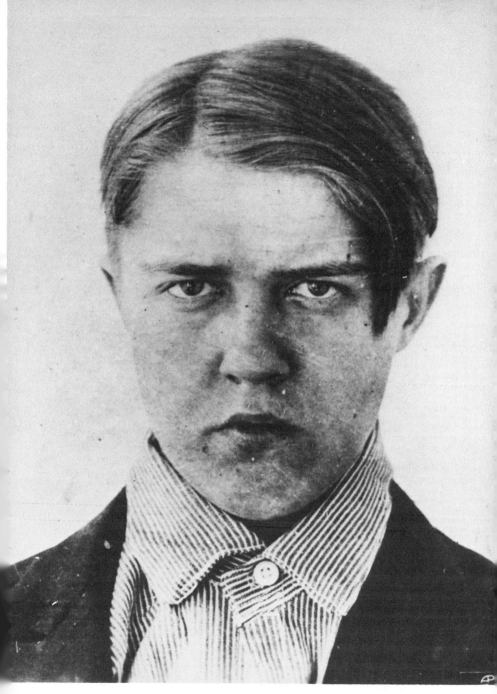

"When I finally got nailed in a burglary I drew a long sentence. There wasn't anything sensational about my arrest. It happened in 1926 when I was eighteen." — ASSOCIATED PRESS

2

"I Was Ten Years Old...and Already on My Way to Being U.S. Public Enemy Number One"

I DON'T BELIEVE there's any such thing as a "born criminal," but I wasn't long out of short pants before I decided on a career in crime. When shady activities first began to appeal to me I was growing up in Topeka, Kansas, in a big old house on Second Street at the edge of town. I lived with my parents, my older sister, and two younger sisters, and while all of them were leading perfectly law-abiding lives, I was hanging out around Kansas Avenue and Fourth Street. The whores and the pimps and the petty gamblers used to operate in that area, and I picked up the occasional dollar and had a lot of fun running errands for them. I just naturally liked the action. I was ten years old, and I guess I was already on my way to being U.S. Public Enemy Number One.

Actually, I wasn't an American then and never did become a citizen. I was a Canadian, which is why the U.S. government deported me to Canada when they finally sprung me from prison in 1969. I was born in Montreal, Quebec. My parents, John and Anna Karpowicz, were Lithuanians, and they made their way to Topeka by way of London, England, Montreal, and Grand Rapids, Michigan. They had a child in each city—Mihalin in London, me in Montreal, Emily in Grand Rapids, and Clara in Topeka.

Topeka was where my father settled down for a while. The house on Second Street stood two stories high, and out back there was a barn with milking cows and a chicken house that squawked with broilers. My father worked like a slave to make money for my mother and us kids. He ran the farm, if you could distinguish our run-down place with that title, and he also held down a full-time job as a design painter for the Santa Fe Railroad. He never stopped hustling, and he expected the same from his family. In fact, he used to keep a bull whip to prod me along if I wasn't doing my share. He didn't have the same trouble with my sisters. They were honest, hard-working girls. My mother was easier on me than my father was. She was a gentle, kind woman, though I doubt if she ever really understood me. And there was one other adult who left a mark on me in my young days. She was the teacher at Branner Elementary School who just casually changed my name one day from Albin Karpowicz to Alvin Karpis. The new handle, she said, was easier to manage, and it stuck with me, apart from the various aliases I took on for business reasons, for the rest of my life.

The person who left the most lasting impression on me when I was a kid, though, was Arthur Witchey, who was eighteen and arrived in Topeka straight out of reformatory. At ten, I considered him a genuine big shot, and when he asked me if I'd like to break into a grocery store with him, I didn't give it a second thought. Yeah, I said. I was raring to move into what struck me as the major leagues. Running errands for hookers was one thing. Pulling a job was a step up. And it seemed so simple. Arthur and I walked into a grocery store one night, picked the place clean of money and easily disposable merchandise, and slipped away.

Arthur got me launched, and for the next few years I kept up my own one-man crime wave in Topeka. If I saw something I liked in a store window, I just bided my time and after dark, when there was no one around, I'd toss a brick through the window and snatch it. I learned how to keep track of the cops on the downtown beats, how to case stores, how to handle myself. Sure it was penny ante stuff, but I wasn't caught once, and the only thing that ended the spree was my father's decision to move to Chicago.

I was fifteen, and up North I put in a short period of honest work. My father took a job as a janitor. Mihalin got married, and so, after a little while, did Emily, the member of the family I was always closest to. Clara stayed in school, and I worked first as an errand boy and later as a shipping clerk for a drug company. I kept up the straight life for almost two years, until the spring of 1925 when I developed some kind of heart trouble and a doctor told me to find a job that was less of a strain.

What a laugh that was when I think about it now. I had to quit my honest job because it was too much for my health, and I went right back to my criminal ways, which, putting it mildly, can create some slight strain on the heart. I left Chicago in favor of Topeka and hooked up with a friend as inclined to crime as I was. Together we ran a hamburger stand that doubled as a base for peddling illegal booze. We also had a sideline—breaking into warehouses. We didn't care what we stole—tires, candy, pocketknives, anything that happened to be lying around.

The other activity that I devoted my time to in those teen-age years was riding the rails. I loved the sound and the feel of trains. Maybe I drew my love for trains from my childhood when our house on Second Street stood smack up against a railroad right of way. Trains fascinated me and all through my teens I was hopping the freights. I saw an awful lot of the United States, from Iowa south through Missouri, Kansas, Oklahoma, and Arkansas into Louisiana and Mississippi, and from Ohio west through Michigan, Illinois, Wisconsin, and Minnesota and into the Dakotas. The trains ran everywhere in those days and that's where I wanted to go—everywhere.

I knew the railroads better than any ticket agent. I knew all the little details that nonpaying passengers needed to know to make full use of the system. Details like where the Santa Fe Chief stopped for water, where the Golden State slowed for curves, what towns the Katy ran through. I also picked up a good deal of valuable information about the towns and villages that lay along the rail lines. I knew, for instance, which places had the best clothing stores and which had the busiest automobile showrooms. That sort of information was handy for a fellow who had settled on a career in crime.

It was on a train that I ran into my first serious trouble with the law. It was in Van Buren, Arkansas, and it was with a railroad bull. He was known as the toughest bull in that part of the country and his hobby was shaking down boxcars for bums. I didn't wait for him to shine his flashlight on me. I jumped down out of that boxcar and blasted away as I ran.

Later I was nailed for riding the roof of the Pan American into Florida and got myself a thirty-day stretch on a chain gang. I can't say it was fun, but nobody clubbed me. I came through unscathed except for one thing: I acquired a prison record. So, when I finally got nailed in a burglary, I drew a long sentence.

There wasn't anything sensational about my arrest. It happened in 1926 when I was eighteen. I was pulling a strictly routine warehouse job in a little town in Kansas. I was just looking around for something worthwhile when the police moved in and took me by surprise. So did the judge when I appeared in court a few days later. He had a long look at me, saw that I'd done time before, and handed me a five-to-ten-year sentence in the reformatory in Hutchinson, Kansas.

I didn't expect such a stiff sentence, but I recognized an opportunity when I saw one: I was about to begin my education in big-time crime.

Hutchinson was a rotten place. It stank. You could never get the smell of dirty socks and spoiled food out of your nose. And the beds crawled. The guards were always shaking you down. If you gave any of them a little back talk, they locked you up in solitary, in the hole. I spent a lot of hours in the hole. But the good side of Hutchinson, for me and my ambitions, was the education I got. I met Lawrence Devol there and a lot of other guys who were willing to pass on the experiences they'd picked up over the years.

The glamor guys of crime in those days were the burglars, with bank burglars at the very top. Devol was a master when it came to breaking into banks. He could handle nitroglycerine, which was a very tricky deal, and he knew a lot about breaking into safes. He specialized in night jobs. When he was given the hours needed at night to crack a safe, he could do it. And that, of course, was a far different proposition from busting into banks and holding them up in the daylight. On those occasions (like the Concordia job later on) you didn't have time to break open the safe without the cooperation of bank employees.

Devol and I slept in neighboring cells at Hutchinson, and we'd spend hours talking. I did most of the listening—and learning. Even though he was only about twenty-five, Devol had been around, and I looked up to him. Partly it was because I was young and a little guy. I stood only about five feet six and never weighed more than 120 pounds. And partly it was because I envied his experience. When he told me about breaking into boxes, the burglar's word for safes, about picking a lock as fast as an ordinary guy could open it with a key, about breaking down a lever-action gun to fit into a suitcase, well, I was all ears.

Our talks went on for almost three years, and then, in the spring of 1929, the idea gradually dawned on us that we ought to break out of Hutchinson. We recruited two other guys to help us, and the whole operation turned out to be a picnic. We chose a likely escape route through the re-formatory garage where we all worked, smuggled a couple of saws out of the prison workshop, sawed through a set of bars one night, and then just lit out across Kansas, stealing cars, clothes, and whatever else we needed as we traveled.

Devol and I split off from the other two, and it was plenty exciting to be on the move with him. He had a classy, easy freedom about him that appealed to me. He'd ask me, for instance, how I'd like a nice new Hickey-Freeman suit, and then we'd break into a haberdashery and come out with a couple of suits apiece, matching shirts and ties and socks and, maybe, for good measure, two brand-new Gladstone bags to carry the stuff in. We stole only the best guns too— rifles, shotguns, 380 Savage automatic pistols—and we'd travel through the countryside in fine big sedan cars, all stolen, of course.

Gradually, we picked our way across Kansas and into Colorado. Being free again was wonderful. Everywhere we went, people were singing "Ramona" and, Jesus, that song got to me and I hummed right along with them. In Limon, Colorado, they were showing Vitaphone pictures, and Devol and I went to one of them. We didn't care about the syn-chronization. You know, so the hero's lips *didn't* move as he sang "Avalon." Who cared!

In Pueblo, we stole a Studebaker and drove through the melon country. In a month or so things would be booming, but right now it was quiet. We rode down through Rocky Ford into Lamar, which would forever be remembered as

Jake Fleagle's town. The Fleagle Gang had had one hell of a shoot-out there and several people, including a bank manager, had been killed. I knew enough history to know this had been one of the hottest bank robberies in the United States.

Then one day we crossed the line into Oklahoma. It was wild and desolate country, that northwestern strip sandwiched in between Kansas, Colorado, New Mexico, and Texas. The dust hadn't started yet, but it was late March and the wind was already blowing. Devol was home and he was glad. He chose Woodward as our first stop. This was a Saturday night kind of town. It was the place the farmers of the region came to whoop it up. And how lucky could you be? We arrived on a Saturday night. We only had a dollar between us, but that didn't bother Devol.

"You know what?" he said as we walked around town. "I got a feeling Oklahoma is going to be good for us."

It's funny how sometimes you just know you're going to like a place. Well, I had that feeling about Oklahoma.

Oklahoma had been a lawless place when it was a territory. Criminals of all kinds drifted there because they knew the only people they had to watch out for were United States marshals. There was no other law. In 1907 the territory became a state, but many of the kids growing up there were the children of outlaws and they hadn't been encouraged to have friendly dealings with the police. These kids had children and they grew up with the same ideas. Pretty soon Oklahoma got to be known as a place where people didn't care too much for law enforcement agencies.

All of this thrilled me. I had read so much about crime in Oklahoma and so many of the guys I had known in Hutchinson had been Oklahomans. Now, to think I was finally there. Jesus, anybody I spoke to might have gone there to escape arrest. Or their parents or grandparents might have been on the lam.

Devol was anxious to go to work, so we broke into a hardware store and got ourselves a set of tools. The next day we went to Alva and stole guns and a little money for expenses. Devol was a cool character and I enjoyed working with him. Passing through Enid, for instance, he looked at me and shook his head. "A hot town," he said. "We don't fool around here." He had got time out of this town once and didn't want to press his luck. Ironically enough, seven years later he was killed right there in Enid by the chief of police. It hadn't been one-sided, though. Devol had killed two cops himself.

The way Devol moved, the cops would have had a hell of a time tracking us. We traveled to Perry, where we ditched our Studebaker, then we took the train to Guthrie. Getting a car was easy in a town full of wealthy oilmen. We stole a Franklin limousine, Devol picked the ignition, and we were off to Tulsa.

In Tulsa we stayed for a while with his folks and then with one of his brothers, Clarence, who made his living holding up rich kids on the city's lovers' lanes on Saturday nights. Clarence struck me as slightly crazy. I didn't mind pulling a gun on a store owner, as Devol and I had done a couple of times. At least in a store you could expect to come away with some worthwhile cash, but with Clarence's system, it was all risk and not much reward. I was learning.

A couple of times during that year, 1929, Devol and I interrupted our travels to go to Chicago and check on the opportunities for easy money. One of the visits didn't do Devol any good. The police picked him up and hauled him back to Hutchinson. As for me, I wasn't nabbed but I did come in for plenty of grief when I paid a visit to my parents. My father kept on insisting that I give myself up, finish out my prison sentence, and start a new life with my mother and him.

"What you're doing is no good," he said to me over and

over again. "You'll be a wanted man all your life if you don't straighten out."

Actually my father's talk made some impression on me. With Devol back in prison and with no one to travel with, I did take a job for a while at Becker's Bakery on the North Side. My parents were delighted. I was a baker's helper and they thought I was ready to settle down. Then old man Becker began losing money on the stock market and decided he could get along without a helper. It was welcome news. I was getting restless again. I spun out of Chicago, stealing and robbing.

The only trouble with my life at that point was that it seemed like a long string of small deals. Nothing big happened. I'd meet up with a guy and we'd stick up a filling station attendant. Or we'd steal a car. Or break into a drugstore, take some narcotics, and peddle them to addicts. Money came and went. Sometimes I'd find myself short and no jobs to pull in sight, and I'd have to wire my sister Emily in Chicago for a loan. She always came through, but I didn't like asking her, not when I was supposed to be making my own way. I wasn't disillusioned. Just impatient for a chance to move into a higher class of crime.

I sputtered through the rest of 1929, not amounting to a hell of a lot, and then Devol returned to the outside world to liven up the action. He'd been transferred from Hutchinson to Lansing, a Kansas prison where you could have time knocked off your sentence if you worked in the coal mine. Devol went into the mine and got out early, and right away he proposed a job aimed at brightening things up for the friends he'd made in Lansing. The guys back there needed clothes, he said. In Lansing, prisoners were allowed to hang onto their own shirts and shoes, but they had no way of replacing clothes that wore out. Devol's idea was to break into a rag joint (he didn't call it a haberdashery) and ship the loot back to his friends.

It was a hell of a lark. Devol chose this store in the Oklahoma town of Bristow, and late one Sunday night we went in through the skylight. We spent four whole hours in the place. Devol had a long list of suit, shoe, and hat sizes, color preferences, and general inclinations in taste for a couple of dozen Lansing prisoners, and we were like a couple of clerks hustling around selecting merchandise for our customers. There were Gladstone bags in the store and we filled up eight of them and wrapped some extra stuff in a big drape. By the time we had it all loaded into our car—also stolen, as usual—we could hardly see out the rear window.

Back at our hotel, we unloaded the clothes and separated them into individual piles for each of Devol's friends. We bundled them in strong wrapping paper, glued labels on, licked on the correct amount of postage, and with everything neatly printed, *except a return address,* we shipped them off to Lansing. We felt pretty happy when we'd finished our good deed—even happier some months later when we learned that every parcel got to its destination. And, oh, yeah, we also held onto a few of those fancy duds for our own wardrobes.

In our second stint, Devol and I pulled a number of jobs in Oklahoma and Kansas, and most of them came out pretty successfully. I remember one night burglary we pulled at a Chrysler agency in Sapulpa, Oklahoma, though, where we came away with a measly eighty bucks and then read in the paper next day that the agency owner was claiming an $800 loss. The chiseler was obviously trying to take his insurance company for a ride. There were crooks everywhere you looked in those days.

I still looked up to Devol and always let him be leader. But something about him was beginning to shake me up a little. For instance, there was the incident at the drugstore in Perry, Oklahoma. He was on his own, without me, and he told me that after he'd broken into the store, he heard somebody out in the alley at the back calling to him to come out with his hands up. Well, according to Devol, instead of looking for a way to sneak out, he burst into the alley blasting with his forty-five automatic. And he left one guy lying on the ground with blood spurting out of a hole in his neck. Devol figured he caught the fellow in the jugular vein, and he had a real gleam in his eye when he told the story.

Not many weeks later, again when I wasn't with him, Devol stirred up even more serious trouble. He and a tough character named Dago Howard beat a box in a combination pool hall and restaurant in Lexington, Missouri. After the robbery, a cop jumped them in an alley. There was a shoot-out and Devol killed the cop. It crossed my mind a few times that maybe I wasn't playing it smart to hang out with Devol after the killing. A cop murderer is a number one target for other policemen. But I didn't desert him.

Times were hard in the early weeks of 1930. Hardly a boxcar rolled through Oklahoma, Missouri, and Nebraska without its quota of unemployed guys heading for new territory to find work. And if Devol wasn't exactly hitting the jackpot with his scores, he was at least getting us enough money to keep going.

"It's tough," Devol said one day, bemoaning the fact that there was so little money in the places we broke into. "But we're making out and that's what counts."

Devol wasn't going to let the Depression get him down. He was always planning something. That's why, toward the end of March, 1930, we hit out for Kansas City. He had set up a downtown poolroom. The job was organized for a Sunday night, and that afternoon, a warm, sunny spring one, we took our car out just to relax. We had some tools in the back of the car—a sharp punch to break through the safe and a hammer to pound the punch. The hammer was a work of art. It was made from a long section of pipe with a hole drilled in it and a piece of gas pipe, maybe half an inch in diameter, inserted in the hole. We had filled the gas pipe with lead because we figured it dulled the sound.

Anyway, we were driving along McGee Boulevard in Kansas City with the tools in the back and Devol in front, bitching about the stomachache he'd got from drinking moonshine the night before, when I looked in my rearview mirror. Cops! I don't know what attracted them, but there they were —two motorcycle cops bearing down on us. They pulled our car over and put us through some preliminary palaver. Devol and I gave them phony names and laid on some fancy story to explain why we were in Kansas City.

"What do you do for a living?" one cop asked Devol.

"I'm a plumber," he answered.

"Let's see your hands."

Devol's hands were thick with calluses from punching safes. But his fingernails were longer than a girl's.

"Are you kidding?" the cop said. "A plumber with fingernails like them?"

The cop began searching the back seat and right away found the tools. He had no doubt what they were for. Both cops then whipped out their pistols, and we were off to the police station.

What happened at the station, to make matters brief, was that the Kansas City police beat the hell out of us. They thought they had hold of a couple of big-time criminals. They thought we'd been breaking into safes all over the city that winter. We hadn't, of course, but we had plenty of other things to hide, and both Devol and I tried to hand the cops wrong names and phony stories. It was no use because they had time and muscle on their side. And they knew one or two painful tactics. They were trying to make me confess to all of the Kansas City safe jobs, and this one hefty cop had a trick of putting four pencils between all the fingers and thumb of one of my hands and then squeezing as hard as he could. Then he'd stand behind me and press his thumbs with all his might behind my ears. Everything he did hurt like hell. The other cops weren't so scientific—they just hauled off and smacked me in the face.

The beatings went on all Sunday night and into the morning without either me or Devol owning up to anything much. The third-degree stuff finally stopped for a very simple reason: A detective came on duty who recognized me as Alvin Karpis, the guy who'd escaped a five-to-ten-year sentence at Hutchinson the year before. What was the use? They had me. I admitted who I was and got sent back to Hutchinson, where the doc said I'd probably lose all my front teeth and that in a matter of days I'd turn every color of the rainbow from the waist up. My ears were already black as coal.

"They really worked them over," the guard who returned me said. "They tell me Karpis and Devol took the worst beatings the cops ever gave anybody in Kansas City."

I went back to Hutchinson to finish out my old sentence plus a little extra for escaping but with no added time for the jobs I pulled during my year of freedom. The cops didn't nail me for any of them and they didn't pin the cop killing in Lexington on Devol either. I returned to Hutchinson with a few different attitudes than I'd had my first time around. I hated cops. That was number one. And I was more determined than ever to make myself into a top-notch, and rich, criminal. I wasn't a killer. At least, I didn't feel like one. Certainly I approved of guns for putting muscle into stickups, and I didn't mind using a few shots to scare off cops or even to wing a guy. But I didn't look to killing as a way of getting kicks the way Devol did. I was anxious to make a pro of myself. The professional quality meant a lot to me. And I wanted to make myself some money. First of all, though, I had to get the hell out of Hutchinson.

3

"Well I Don't Care: All the Banks Ever Do Is Foreclose on Us Farmers"

ON MAY 2, 1931, I WALKED out of prison a free man, not on parole but with a full discharge. It was a beautiful morning and I was decked out in a Stetson hat and Florsheim shoes and, all things considered, feeling pretty good.

How did I get out so quickly? It was simple, really. I just followed Devol's earlier example, got myself transferred from Hutchinson to the Kansas State Penitentiary in Lansing and went to work in the coal mines. I had to work like hell, but I managed to earn a lot of time to be credited against my sentence.

The coal mine wasn't easy to take. They gave you hunks of bread that you dipped in syrup and you had to fight the flying cockroaches that were blind from the darkness and kept zooming into the syrup. But you learned from the experienced men to pick them out and then to gulp the food.

I don't know which were worse, the roaches or the mules. The mules were blind, too, and you had to bribe them just to walk by. Otherwise, they'd bite or kick you. Sometimes we gave them bread but oftener it was the chewing tobacco the institution reserved for the inmates. The guys took all they could of the stuff and the officials must have thought there was a lot of chewing going on in the mine. There was, but the mules were doing most of it.

I worked hard, but I was lucky too. For instance, some of the long-termers in the mine weren't interested in accumulating time, preferring money instead. They agreed to donate some time to me. It seemed kind of impossible to me, but after two months in the mine, I learned that I had earned 180 days. Not bad for two months' work.

Coal mine, did I say? It was a gold mine.

Apart from work, life in Lansing was bearable. I had considerable prestige in the joint because of the clothes Devol and I had shipped in to the guys. Then there were the friendships I made. Well, business relationships maybe. There were guys like Freddie Barker. I met Freddie in Lansing, liked him, and planned to team up with him in the free world.

My very first meeting with Freddie was an unforgettable event, not because it was all that dramatic, but just because it was so pleasant. On one of my first nights in the place I was on my way to dinner, when a guy stopped me at the door to the mess hall. He was short, not more than five feet four, maybe twenty-seven years old, and he had sandy hair, a nice grin, and a mouthful of gold teeth. He stuck his hand out.

"I'm Freddie Barker," he said. "I already know who you are. Let's go in to supper together."

I'd heard plenty about Freddie over the years. I knew that he came out of the Ozarks and that he was very capable with a gun or a safe. I'd also heard a few things about his older brother, Herman. Herman was another tough operator. He'd been killed in 1927 while beating it with two other guys from a holdup of an icehouse in Newton, Kansas. Some cops stopped them near Wichita. One cop leaned down to look in Herman's car window, and Herman clutched the cop around the neck and fired a Luger into his head. A cop on the other side of the car opened up on Herman and shot so many bullets into him that Herman turned his Luger on himself and finished the job.

Freddie had a lot of rough times in his background, but he was always as cheerful and friendly as he was at our first meeting. He appreciated the help I'd given Devol in shipping the new clothes in, but that wasn't the only basis for our friendship. The truth was that we just hit it off from the start.

After dinner that first night, Freddie and a couple of others took me into the yard. Freddie was carrying a Prince Albert tobacco can, and when he opened it, the thing was overflowing with marijuana. He told me that they grew it on the prison farm on an island in the Missouri River. It sprung up in such huge crops that any prisoner could buy a full Prince Albert can for only twenty-five cents from the cons who tended it. Freddie spread his can around and we all lit up. The marijuana took ten minutes to hit me. Then I couldn't stop giggling.

"For chrissake," I said, "it's more fun in here than on the street."

Freddie knew his way around Lansing. He'd been in the place since 1926 on a five-to-ten-year burglary sentence. He'd beaten a box in Windfield, Kansas, and was making his escape, when a townsman spotted him and knocked him cold with a brick.

Freddie did his best to make his stay in Lansing comfortable. He arranged a transfer for me to his cell, and when I arrived, I was impressed, to say the least, with his writing table and bookshelf and his stock of canned sardines, jams, and crackers. And there were other surprises. Freddie used to set up lunches in the yard—I don't know how—that featured treats like canned chicken, fresh bread, and pies and pastries. Freddie liked his luxuries, and he was a generous host.

Freddie was tougher and more experienced than I was, and I thought of him as a kind of leader when we met later by arrangement in Joplin, Missouri, to join a number of friends and guys we'd known in prison and knock off some jewelry and clothing shops. They were all nighttime jobs, all in towns in Missouri and Kansas and other Midwest states. And we didn't get rich off any of them.

My life in crime was still minor-league stuff, though, and to make matters just a little worse, all of us were being more harassed by cops in every town we stopped in than I'd ever experienced before. The police nailed Freddie on a solid case and shipped him off to jail in Claremore, Oklahoma, to await trial. He escaped almost immediately, but I lost track of him for a few weeks, and I spent the time without him shuffling from one small potatoes job to another.

Then, one day in the fall of 1931, Freddie reappeared in Tulsa, where I was hanging out, and proposed a bank holdup. He looked different. He was nothing but skin and bones, and his face showed he was on the lam. His eyes kept shifting, his cheeks were thin, and his jawbones stuck out. But he was the same hard-rock Freddie I'd met and liked in prison.

"I know a bank in Mountain View, Missouri," he said. "It's easy to take."

"All right," I said, "if we're going to make money, I'm interested. I'm sick of beating boxes for a few bucks. I'm for the bank. But if we're just going to screw around, I'm going back to Chicago."

I meant it. I was fed up with missing out on the big money.

Freddie was serious too. He'd stuck up many banks before, and he was ready to lead me on my first daytime bank job.

The Mountain View plan took four men, and Freddie and I included a couple of ex-cons named Bill Weaver and Jimmie Wilson. The idea was for me and Weaver to break into the bank at three in the morning and wait until the employees arrived.

Well, the preliminaries went off without a hitch, so neatly in fact that Weaver lay down on a table in the conference room where we were waiting it out and fell asleep. Just before nine in the morning, we heard two employees come in. We tied handkerchiefs over our faces and held our guns ready. Then this pretty girl stepped across the entrance, looked at the guns and the handkerchiefs, and nearly died on the spot.

Weaver grabbed her. She let out a squawk and I ran down the hall into the main banking area, yelling "Don't move! We're robbing this place!"

We got one of the employees to open the vault, and Weaver and I scooped up all the money inside, shoved the employees into the vault, left it unlocked, and told them not to make a move for ten minutes.

Freddie had the car idling and we spun down the main road sprinkling two-inch roofing tacks on the road to discourage the cops who might follow us. When we were far enough away, we counted the money. It came to damn near $7,000.

My first daylight bank job—and not a hitch in the whole operation.

Well, the experience boosted my confidence and I was anxious to get into more bank work. But I had to wait awhile, maybe three or four months. Other things kept getting in the way. For one thing, Freddie was so hot around Missouri and Oklahoma that we decided to pick up and move to the St. Paul area where the atmosphere was more relaxed and the cops would leave us alone.

The action was brisk in Minnesota, but none of it involved bank stickups. After all, most of the other guys still considered me a kid, and they weren't sure I was ready to crash the bigger banks. I played my part in plenty of other jobs, though, like the time we looted a whole town. It was Cambridge, Minnesota, and Freddie and I and another guy arrived late one night, took the only town cop a prisoner, and proceeded to move up one side of the main street and down the other looting every store as we went. We beat a couple of safes, helped ourselves to some clothes, appliances, and other stuff, and picked out a nice four-door sedan from a Buick agency to get us out of town.

We stole a lot of cigarettes on various jobs for resale at cut-rate prices. We stole so many cartons, in fact, that at one point I thought we'd cornered the cigarette market for the entire state of Minnesota. We handled other jobs, breaking into safes and stores and warehouses. And once I was included in on a booze job.

Jack Peifer gave us the job, and this was quite an honor because he was a big man around the Twin Cities. For one thing, he was tied into the Minneapolis gambling interests through people like Tommy Banks, Jack Davenport, and Benny Harris. Then Prohibition opened up a whole new field for him. He was bringing booze down from Canada to keep the speakeasies around St. Paul supplied, and this time he had paid a train crew to spot a boxcar full of the stuff on a siding near Minneapolis. But he wanted a couple of guys who could handle themselves to watch the transfer from boxcar to trucks—just in case the cops or rival thugs showed up.

The unloading went off perfectly and Peifer was pleased. So was I. I was getting a reputation.

Then came a branch of the Northwestern National Bank in Minneapolis. I was twenty-four years old and figured at the time that I had come of age. I'd waited until the winter of 1932, but finally I was set for my first genuine major stickup. It was a big bank and a big score, and Freddie asked me to go along.

There were five of us in on it, Freddie and me, two pros named Tommy Holden and Phil Courtney, and my wild friend Devol, who'd joined us in St. Paul around the New Year full of stories of shootings and holdups and killings. It was Devol's idea to use a big car in honor of the big job. So we stole a luxury Lincoln with a gorgeous interior and drove up to the Northwestern National.

We parked in the alley behind the bank. Holden stayed with the car. The other four of us walked in the front door. Courtney took charge of the lobby. Devol, Freddie, and I moved in to clean out the cages. We were all waving guns, and with Freddie and Devol yelling out the instructions, none of the customers or employees made a false move. The bank had big walk-in vaults. Freddie and Devol took them while I helped Courtney cover the lobby. I noticed that Courtney was doing a lot of gabbing with a pretty switchboard operator. I thought he should tend to business, but I was the junior on the job and so I kept my mouth shut.

Freddie and Devol moved quickly into the vault with the head cashier, forcing him to open the seven individual safes. They were calm, quiet, efficient, and smooth. I was impressed by the way they operated. They scooped money out of the drawers and shelves and dropped it quickly into laundry bags we'd carried into the bank. In a couple of minutes they'd finished with the vault and Devol looked out a window onto the main street.

"Watch it. The cops are unloading at both ends of the block!"

While the police headed for the front door, we went out the back. Holden was standing in the alley with his gun out. He had a detective up against the wall, and he had the detective's gun in his own pocket. We piled into the car and ripped out onto the main street. No one stopped us. Evidently, the guy Holden had nailed was the only cop who'd thought to check the back door, and we pulled away from the bank without firing or ducking a shot.

Back at the house we'd rented in St. Paul, the five of us counted out the money. It added up to more loot than I'd ever seen in my life—over $75,000 in paper money, another $6,500 in coins, and $185,000 in bonds. And we could have taken even more as we discovered when we read the evening papers. The job was headline material in all the Minneapolis-St. Paul dailies, and they reported everything in detail, including the news that while Courtney was busy gabbing with the pretty switchboard operator, a teller a few feet away managed to stuff $10,000 in hundred-dollar bills into his pockets.

After my Minneapolis coming out, the bank jobs came fast and heavy. We ranged all over the Midwest through most of 1932, knocking over banks in places like Fort Scott, Kansas, and Concordia, Kansas, Beloit, Wisconsin, Flandreau, South Dakota, Redwood Falls, Minnesota, and Wahpeton, North Dakota, and a whole slew of other such towns. I almost always worked with Freddie and Devol plus one or two other guys we'd pick up, depending on the size of the job. We made a lot of money, but we worked hard for it. Every score had its special problems and each its special surprises.

On the Fort Scott job, for instance, a lot of crises turned up that we didn't count on. It started smoothly enough. There were six of us in on it—Freddie, Devol, and I, Courtney and Holden from the Northwestern National job, and another pro named Harvey Bailey.

Devol and Courtney went in first, then Freddie, then Bailey and me, and we surprised the hell out of everybody in there. Two tellers just dropped to the floor. One of them reached for an alarm button and I kicked his hand. Bailey and I kept our guns up. The other three crammed the cash into some barracks bags. It was going neatly. We even collared an extra $800 when a messenger from the local light and power company strolled in with a bank deposit.

Then all hell broke loose. One of the employees must have hit an alarm. The street outside suddenly filled with people and there were cops and sheriff's men heading straight for the bank. Devol hustled out with two bags of loot. Holden pulled up in the Hudson and tossed me a machine gun, and I held it ready. Courtney, Bailey, and Freddie all grabbed girls for hostages. Courtney didn't get far with his. The girl was so scared that she squatted down on the sidewalk and pissed. We slung the other two on the running boards, one on each side, and Holden hit the accelerator hard.

None of the cops on foot in front of the bank used their guns for fear of hitting the girls, but we weren't far out of town when we realized we'd picked up a tail. It was a motorcycle policeman and we needed to shake him. We'd run the roads a few days earlier and plotted a careful route across country, and we didn't need a dumb cop to give it away. We slowed up every time we dipped over a hill and waited for him to turn up behind us. We were ready to greet him with rifle fire. But he was cagey. He'd wait until we appeared over the next hill before he'd come on. Courtney got mad and fired a few shots from the moving car. They hit nothing except dust, but finally we got rid of him just by turning on the speed. All the dust and wind, though, were tough on those girls hanging onto the running boards for dear life through the entire course. When we let them off on the roadside in the middle of nowhere, they were properly grateful.

We were kind of grateful ourselves. We made $47,000 out of the Fort Scott job.

Strange things were always happening in our business, however, and later on the day of the Fort Scott robbery, three men were arrested on a side road in Missouri. They had shotguns and pistols and their Buick was stolen. The cops immediately announced they had captured the guys who robbed our bank. They were Jim Clark, Ed Davis, and Frank Sawyer, escapees from the Oklahoma State Penitentiary in McAlester. Bank employees and people on the street identified them and, Jesus, that got me. People sure reacted strangely in situations like that. I'm sure they thought they were making accurate identifications. The cops didn't find any money on those three guys, but they just ignored that aspect of it.

Clark, Davis, and Sawyer were given twenty to a hundred years in Lansing, and less than a year afterward they all escaped. Clark and Davis were nailed on other beefs later. Clark went to Alcatraz and Davis to Folsom. Davis didn't like Folsom, made a break for it, and was killed.

Sawyer was picked up a few weeks after he broke out of Lansing and was sent to McAlester, from which he had escaped before the Fort Scott job. He remained in McAlester until 1962, when he was returned to Lansing to finish his other sentence. It was a long stretch on a bum rap, but soon after my own parole in 1969, I went to bat for him. I sent an affidavit to the governor of the state of Kansas stating that Sawyer was innocent of the Fort Scott robbery and explaining the real circumstances. Sawyer got a full pardon.

The bank at Wahpeton, North Dakota, looked like a strictly routine job. Freddie, Jess Doyle, Freddie's brother Doc, Devol, and I went on it. We didn't spend more than six or seven minutes clearing out the cash, but as we reached the back door, Jess Doyle, the outside man, hollered that cops were covering both ends of the alley. We turned back into the bank, grabbed two girls, and headed back to the car with them as shields. The cops held fire when they saw the girls on the running boards, but as soon as we cleared the alley, girls or no girls, they opened up at our rear tires. They were shooting buckshot and the stuff rained on the back of the car like hailstones. And one of the cops must have been a marksman, because by the time we got to the edge of town, both back wheels were running on the rims and the fender wells were a tinny mess.

The girls on the running boards kept screaming. One of them tried to jump as we bounced along the road at fifty miles an hour. Devol leaned out the window and grabbed her around the waist. We swung onto a side road and almost ran down a posse that was organizing to cut us off. They didn't shoot when they saw the girls and we thought we were out of it safe. But when we were a hundred yards down the road, one guy in the posse let fly with a high-powered rifle. The first shots hit the rear of the car. The next hit one of the girls.

She screamed hysterically. We kept going. There was no way we were going to stop with the posse back down the road. We gunned the car for another two miles until we hit a prearranged turnoff point into a farmer's field. With the girl yelling herself hoarse, we bounced across the pasture, ran through a dry creek bed, and pulled up at a little schoolhouse, where we jumped out and looked at the wounded girl. The sniper's bullet had broken her leg.

"Just go away!" the other girl screamed. "Don't stay! They'll start shooting at us again!"

I told her to shut up, and I took our medicine kit out of the car. I put a quarter-grain of morphine into the syringe and shot the whole load into a muscle in the wounded girl's arm. I told her that the morphine would take care of her pain, and I told the other girl not to blame us, that they could blame the trigger-happy bastard who fired at the car. Then we took off again, leaving the girls at the schoolhouse.

We made about a mile on the rims. The car was rattling like it was going to fly into a million pieces when we pulled into a farmyard beside an ancient dilapidated house. An old

Essex sat in the yard. Four or five kids came out to look us over, followed by their mother, then by the farmer of the place himself. I pointed to the Essex and asked him if it'd run.

"Yeah, it'll run," he said, with a kind of blank look on his face. "It doesn't have hardly any brakes and there's kind of a short in the wiring, but it'll run some." Then he looked around at our car and looked closer at us. "What's this here all about?"

"We just robbed the Wahpeton bank," I told him, "and we need a car to get out of here fast. We're taking yours and leaving ours and we'll give you some money to square it."

Devol pulled some bills out of the bag, and you could tell from the look on the farmer's face that he didn't want to delay us.

"You robbed the bank, did you?" he said. "Well, I don't care. All the banks ever do is foreclose on us farmers."

We climbed into the Essex and moved out of the district in a big hurry. And later on we divided up our $7,000 take.

4

"That Was My Friend Freddie Barker. All Business"

THE WAY FREDDIE BARKER handled the Doc Moran matter probably told as much about the kind of guy Freddie was as any other single thing in his life. Doc Moran was a threat. He turned out to have the worst vice anybody in our business could have: He talked too much. And it took somebody who was efficient and cold and expert to look after him. Somebody like Freddie.

Doc Moran was a real doctor. His name was Joseph P. Moran, and he was a fairly intelligent, clean-cut fellow in his late thirties who practiced out of a hotel on Irving Park Boulevard in Chicago. He had good connections with labor racketeers around the city, and he performed quite a few abortions in his time. In fact, he put in some time in Joliet for one abortion job the cops nailed him on.

51

Freddie and I went to Moran for another of his medical specialties, fingerprint removing. Freddie and I were very hot at the time, the spring of 1934. The cops figured us for a lot of bank robberies, shoot-ups, and other jobs, and we thought we'd make their work tougher if we didn't have fingerprints to leave around. We knew Moran by reputation, and he agreed to look after us. It'd cost Freddie $500 and me $750. The extra $250 was for patching up my face from the going-over the Kansas City police gave it back in 1930.

The fingerprint operation was damned painful. Moran started by looping elastic bands tight around my fingers at the first joints. Next he froze my fingertips with an injection of cocaine in each one. Finally he started the scraping. He used a scalpel, sharpening the ends of my fingers just like you'd sharpen a pencil. He really took the meat off, and as he finished each finger, he'd remove the elastic band and bandage cotton around the scraped tip.

The operation on my face wasn't nearly as tough, partly because Moran put me right out with a hefty shot of morphine. When I came to, Moran said all the operations had been successes as far as he was concerned. Freddie and I weren't so sure. Freddie had a lot of pain right from the start, and one of his thumbs became infected and swelled into a pulpy mess. I didn't complain at first, but after a few weeks, I developed some ugly scars on my face that refused to heal.

Still, Doc Moran was the least of our worries. We had to keep on a constant lookout for the cops, and Freddie and I decided life would be simpler outside Chicago. We chose Toledo and settled in an apartment house with some friends. One was a stickup man named Harry Campbell, who had the dumb luck one day to get bitten by a Chinese chow. He started hollering about rabies and demanding a doctor. And that chow bite brought Doc Moran back into our lives. We didn't want to risk calling in a local doctor, and the

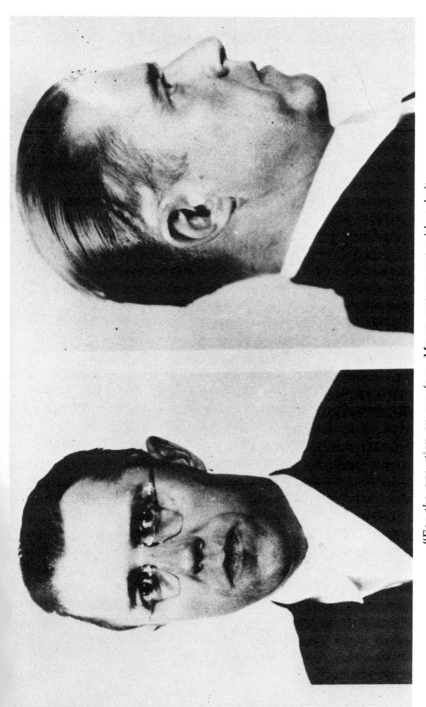

"For the operation on my face, Moran put me out with a hefty shot of morphine. When I came to, Moran said all the operations had been success as far as he was concerned. Freddie and I weren't so sure." — U.S. DEPARTMENT OF JUSTICE

only alternative was to import Moran, so Doc Barker, who was also hiding out with us, hustled off to Chicago and returned with Moran, and Harry Campbell got his anti-rabies shot.

Moran didn't leave Toledo after he'd finished the job we hired him for, though. Instead, he hung around, did a lot of heavy drinking and chased after girls, bragging about his medical talents. As far as Freddie and I were concerned, Doc Moran was turning into a menace. He was a lush and talkative and the whole situation hit the crisis point one night when a whorehouse madam we knew told us that he'd been talking up a storm with a couple of her girls. He'd let it out that he was a big doctor from Chicago and that he could erase men's fingerprints and change their appearances.

Freddie didn't say a word. He sat down in a chair in the apartment. He didn't speak to me. He didn't tell me what was on his mind. He looked straight ahead. And after a while he went to bed.

Freddie was in and out of the apartment over the next couple of days. So was I. We had our own business to look after, and I didn't give Doc Moran any thought until a runner arrived from Chicago. Moran was wanted back there for an abortion. Where was he?

"He's probably off on a drunk," one of the guys said.

"Yeah, or he's chasing broads," somebody else volunteered.

Freddie didn't open his mouth. The runner hung around for a few days, then gave up and returned to Chicago without Moran. When he'd gone, Freddie asked me to go for a drive along the Lake Erie shore with him.

He was very cool.

"Doc and I shot the son of a bitch," he said. "Anybody who talks to whores is too dangerous to live. We dug a hole in Michigan and dropped him in and covered the hole with lime. I don't think anybody's ever going to come across Doc Moran again."

"We dug a hole in Michigan and dropped him in. . . . I don't think anybody's ever going to come across Doc Moran again." — UPI

That was my friend Freddie Barker. *All business.* Doc Moran was a threat. He had to go. Freddie took care of it. No fuss or bother, no word to anyone. A job professionally handled. Freddie was like that for as long as I knew him, and though our friendship didn't cover many years, he was probably the friend who was closest to me. We were partners in dozens of jobs; we served time together, dodged the cops together, and lived in the same houses and apartments. We never had a falling out, and our names were joined forever in everybody's minds as the leaders of the Karpis-Barker Gang.

I was never certain when the expression "Karpis-Barker Gang" first registered with the cops and the public and other burglars, but it was natural for us to hook up and we made a great team, as all the successful jobs we engineered together proved. Freddie had a vicious streak, though. I saw many displays of it and heard stories of more in the years after we left Lansing. To be frank, I was sometimes slightly stunned by Freddie's free and easy way with a gun. He never seemed to mind gunning down anybody who stood in his way, whether it was a cop or a hood or an ordinary guy on the street.

I didn't know how to explain Freddie's constant readiness to settle matters with bullets. I supposed the tendency ran in his family. At least his brothers carried on in the same style. Herman Barker died with a gun in his hand, and Doc was also an itchy-finger man. Doc Barker didn't look dangerous. An inch shorter than Freddie, though stockier, he had a neat mustache, a reddish complexion, and black hair combed straight back. But harmless as he may have looked, he was a lethal operator. Before Doc joined Freddie and me in our jobs, he served thirteen years in prison in McAlester, Oklahoma, for the murder of a night watchman during a holdup.

Freddie's violence wasn't just a family habit, though. It

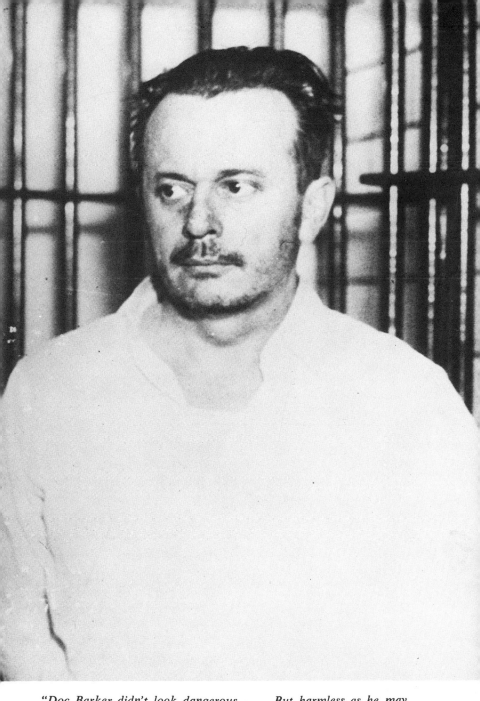

"Doc Barker didn't look dangerous. . . . But harmless as he may have looked, he was a lethal operator." — UPI

also came out of his impatience and his drive to make everything perfect. Freddie liked his bank jobs to run like clockwork. He didn't let me in on the big jobs until he was convinced I could hold up my end. He was right, too. He was always right when it came to planning, directing, and carrying out a holdup, and if anyone disagreed with him or interfered with his thinking, then Freddie removed the guy from any further consideration.

A year or so earlier, after the disposal of Doc Moran, Freddie decided that Jess Doyle, an old friend who often worked with the gang, had to go. On a night shortly after we'd knocked off a big bank in Fairbury, Nebraska, Freddie had walked in on Jess and his girlfriend, a woman named Helen Murray. Jess had a bunch of newspapers from Lincoln and Omaha, Nebraska, spread out on their bed, all open to reports of the Fairbury job. Jess was doing a little bragging. Freddie didn't say a word, but as far as he was concerned, Jess had broken the same rule as Doc Moran: You didn't tell broads about jobs. Not ever. Freddie came to me and said that Jess was out and that if I didn't like it, then it was good-bye to me, too. I didn't like it. Jess was a top operator. But Freddie was the boss, and the two of us advised Jess to get in with another gang. Jess was too close a friend to knock off, even for Freddie.

Cops, of course, were the main people who interfered with Freddie's plans, and he never had second thoughts about blasting them out of the way. It didn't matter where Freddie ran into them—during a job, casing a bank, just ambling down the street. Freddie's attitude was simple: If they were cops and if they might somehow get between him and his work, then he shot them.

An incident in Monett, Missouri, showed Freddie's approach to the whole matter of cops. He and Bill Weaver had broken into a garage to steal a car for a job. Freddie slid behind the wheel and Weaver opened the sliding door to let

Freddie out. As the door moved slowly aside, a cop appeared, standing just beyond the entrance. He had his gun drawn and he was looking at Weaver. Freddie flipped the car lights on. The cop was blinded. Freddie leaned out the window and shot the cop dead.

What did Freddie say later?

"That's what comes from stealing these goddamn cars all the time."

Freddie didn't spend all his time tending to business; only most of it. But he liked his pleasures, too. He and I used to see a lot of movies, when we weren't nervous of being spotted, and we had a lot of fun at the 1933 Chicago World's Fair. Freddie always was fond of good plain food—he didn't see much of it when he was a kid growing up in Oklahoma— and like any other boy from the Midwest, he was a great fisherman and not a bad swimmer. We got in plenty of both when we were between jobs, and Freddie was always a great companion and a guy who liked to laugh.

Girls liked Freddie and he didn't mind spending money on them. But he wasn't always lucky in the type of broad who hooked him. Paula Harmon turned out to be a rotten choice, though you couldn't tell that to Freddie when he got stuck on her. Paula was the widow of Charlie Harmon, who was knocked off in a bank score, and Freddie took up with her in the spring of 1933. He kept her with him, looking after her, buying her stuff, showing her a good time, for over a year. Until Paula blew the whole deal all by herself.

Paula was a drunk. She couldn't stay off the sauce, and one afternoon in the fall of '34 when we were lying low in Cleveland, she and two other broads went out on their own. They started drinking it up in a cocktail lounge, and after a couple of hours they got into a screaming brawl. The lounge owner called the cops, and they hauled those dumb broads off to the station. When the rest of us heard about the pickup, we couldn't afford to hang around. We moved out of Cleve-

Fred Barker Bad Influence on Karpis, Ex-wife Believe

Tulsa, Okla., May 1.—(AP)—In surrendering to federal agents without a fight, Alvin Karpis failed to carry out the boast his former wife, Dorothy Slayman, once heard him make—" I'll never be taken alive."

She won a divorce last Nov. 22, testifying she had not seen him for nearly four years. The decree was granted here on grounds of neglect and cruelty.

After her divorce Karpis' former wife said she planned to continue to attend business college. She has been living quietly here since and could not be located immediately tonight.

"He was young and good looking and I fell for him hard when I met him at a night club," Miss Slayman once said in describing her romance with the man who became known as Public Enemy No. 1.

"He told me he was a jewelry salesman and we ran off to Sapul just west of here, and were marri That was in December, 1931. We w to Chicago. I left him after onl; few months of married life. I ne saw him after that."

Karpis and Freddie Barker, la slain, were believed to have been two men who shot it out with offic at an apartment house here abou month after Miss Slayman and F pis were married. The men escap leaving about $4,000 worth of jewe behind them. The jewelry had b stolen from a store in Henrye Okla.

"It was in Chicago," the forr Mrs. Karpis recalled, "that I he Alvin boast to Freddie Barker t he never would be taken alive. A that he promised me he would straight' but I guess he never di always thought that Freddie Bar was a bad influence on Alvin."

FATHER OF KARPIS WON'T DISCUSS SON UNSEEN FOR YEARS

John Karpaviez, 2842 North Francisco avenue, father of the desperado Alvin Karpis, who was seized in New Orleans yesterday, declined last night to make any comment on the news of his son.

"All I want is to be let alone," he said to callers at his home.

Karpis has not been near the home of his parents in years, according to neighbors who are on good terms with the family.

ORDER PIQUETT SENT TO FEDERA PRISON FRIDA

The United States Circuit Cour Appeals yesterday issued a for mandate denying Attorney L Piquett's appeal from his two prison sentence and $10,000 fine harboring the late Homer Van M Dillinger gangster. Deputy Un States Marshal Joseph Tobin not Piquett, who has been at lib under bond, that he will be sen Leavenworth penitentiary next day. Piquett appealed to the Un States Supreme court from the peals court decision up

"Another thing I always had to keep in the back of my mind was that my great pal Freddie Barker was a natural killer."

land right away, and Freddie never saw Paula the drunk ever again. Freddie might have made mistakes with broads, but he didn't in business. There was an incident down in Arkansas early in our career together that showed the scrupulous way Freddie's mind worked. He and Bill Weaver borrowed my car on a Saturday night to drive around a town called Pocahontas to check out some scores. They'd been rolling around for a couple of hours when Weaver stopped the car and wandered up an alley to take a leak. A cop came by who said he was the night chief. Freddie watched him jot down the license number of the car. When the cop had finished writing, Freddie pulled his forty-five and invited him into the car, relieving him of the notepaper with the license number.

The three of them drove a couple of miles out of Pocahontas and pitch-dark. Freddie pulled the cop out of the car and and stopped by the side of the road. It was around 3 A.M. walked him through the weeds to a gravel pit. Freddie stopped. He told the cop to keep walking. Freddie raised his forty-five and shot the cop four times.

"I did the right thing," Freddie told me later. "The cop had the license number and knew what the car looked like. If we figured on doing a job back in his town, he'd recognize us and the car right away."

We were hoping the body wouldn't be found for a while, but the very next day an old hillbilly woman went back to the gravel pit for a leak and discovered the dead cop. We were worried for a while, but then came the damnedest news. A Pocahontas hillbilly confessed that he had stolen a forty-five automatic from a filling station and that the day chief of police had got him to kill the night chief. Well, now the day chief was in jail, and it looked like the heat was off us.

Freddie was a stickler for thoroughness all right. But another thing I always had to keep in the back of my mind was that *my great pal Freddie Barker was a natural killer.*

5

"Bank Robbery, Dangerous as It Was, Could Get to Be Routine"

You had to be pretty wild and not a little crazy to take a bank like the Third Northwestern National in Minneapolis. It was a triangular building smack on one of the city's busiest streets, with a streetcar stop right in front of it, and practically the whole goddamn place was in glass. It would be like working in a greenhouse, but then we sometimes did things like that deliberately, maybe to inject some extra excitement into our work. Bank robbery, dangerous as it was, could get to be routine.

Freddie's mother was living with us at this time, and the first thing we did in preparation for this caper was to arrange for Ma to go to Chicago for a few days and then on to Reno, where we would meet her. It was now mid-December, 1932, and right after this job we hoped to go to Nevada for the winter.

A gang of us was involved in this one—Freddie, Doc, Jess Doyle, Lawrence Devol, Bill Weaver, a guy named Vern Miller, and me. Jess was elected to drive the car and the rest of us agreed to approach the bank on foot from different directions.

We figured we might get jumped on this one, so we emptied the armory. We had four machine guns, two rifles and, of course, our pistols. We made sure, too, that we had plenty of extra clips. We didn't want to be caught short if the cops moved in.

In this business, though, the unexpected was the rule and not the exception, and two days before the date set for the robbery, there was an urgent call from Ma Barker. She had had heart palpitations and had hit the panic button. One of us had to go to her—and in a hurry. I was the only one who knew my way around Chicago, so I was elected.

The robbery came off on schedule one bitterly cold December afternoon. The guys slammed into the bank brandishing their guns and suddenly everything went crazy. Some customers argued when they were ordered to stay where they were and got slapped. Some of the women took it real hard and started screaming hysterically. Outside, a streetcar pulled up and, Jesus, the motorman dropped to the floor with his hands over his head. The passengers, meanwhile, sat in their seats gawking. The guys were putting on a real show.

Then suddenly, right in the midst of all the commotion, one of the bank tellers dropped to the floor and set off the goddamn alarm.

It was obvious now the fireworks were going to start. Devol put a drum on his machine gun and went into the street just as this squad car whipped up. He began shooting right away and so did Jess and, in a few seconds, the car was riddled with bullets. Then Devol hit a slick bit of pavement, his feet flew out from under him, and he fell on his back. His finger was on the trigger and he was firing like crazy into the sky.

Next the guys discovered that the right rear tire of the jazzy big Lincoln chosen for the caper was flat. Devol must have fired into it as he fell. But they just piled in and Miller, who was one hell of a driver, took over from Jess behind the wheel.

They spun off along a route which, because it had been used so often in getaways, was called Bank Robbers' Row. It was a way of getting from Minneapolis to the twin city of St. Paul without having to cross the bridge where the cops usually set up their roadblocks.

Just inside the city limits of St. Paul, they had parked a second car, a Chevy, in case of emergency, and when they pulled up, some of the guys jumped out got into the Chevy, and followed the Lincoln. Both cars pulled to a stop in Como Park. The tire and rim of the Lincoln's wheel were gone. Vern had been driving over those icy streets at more than sixty miles an hour.

The Chevy had hot plates. These had to be taken off and the right ones put back on. Ignoring little details like that could result in capture. While this was being done, a jalopy came along with two fellows in it. The driver stopped and damn near fell out of the car straining to get a look at the plates on the Chevy.

"Get going," Freddie shouted, "or else."

The guy ignored the warning and Freddie fired. He got him right in the head and the blood streamed out over the side of the car. His friend pulled him across the seat, got behind the wheel himself, and drove off.

The guys finished changing the plates, got back into the Chevy, and everybody headed for Freddie's apartment. They made their getaway, but when they counted the loot, they were in for a bitter disappointment. They had got only

$22,000, a paltry sum in view of the shooting and lives lost, not to mention the loss of the Lincoln. There was usually a postmortem after a caper, and this time there was plenty to discuss. Finally, it was agreed that everybody should blow town for a few months.

"Well," Devol said, "my bags are in the Chrysler and I've got a half-gallon jug of gin and orange juice and I'm ready to roll."

Devol didn't take this thing as seriously as the others. He played it all very cool. Actually, he had killed so many cops that this was just another incident to him.

It was finally decided that Freddie, Doc, Jess, and Bill would drive to Reno in the Chrysler and that Vern would drive the Auburn back to Chicago and get rid of it. As for Devol, he was going to make his own plans. He had managed to work out a deal to spring a guy named Harry Hull out of the Oklahoma penitentiary and he wanted to get him straightened out before doing anything else.

That day the newspapers carried headlines enough to scare you to death. On the front page of one paper was a picture of the two dead cops in the squad car. They had been hit umpteen times.

Then there was this weird story about the two guys in Como Park. When the guy drove off after the shooting, he noticed his friend was still alive. He raced over to the police radio dispatcher's office in panic. The cops knew all about the robbery by this time and when this fellow came in saying there was a guy badly shot-up in the car, they immediately jumped to the conclusion that he was one of the robbers. Well, before he knew what was happening, those cops were on him and they gave him a terrible working over right there in the dispatcher's office. In the meantime, the wounded man in the car died.

The next day Vern Miller joined me in Chicago and we exchanged information. He told me about the fiasco in

Minneapolis and I told him about Ma. She had panicked for nothing. We weren't even sure it had been her heart. It could just as well have been indigestion.

In Chicago, I stayed with Mike Stacci. He was a regular working guy and lived in the Melrose Park area. His cousin, Rocky DeGrazio, handled the slot machines for the Syndicate in the suburbs. Anyway, it was a real safe place to stay because Melrose Park was dominated by the outfit. They had even put in the mayor and chief of police.

I stayed a couple of days longer and then caught a flight for Reno. I wasn't the average tourist. I had guns and clips in my suitcase and a 380 in the waistband of my trousers. United Air Lines' twenty-one-passenger, tri-motored Boeing was the first commercial airliner I had ever been on. I was slightly tense. But a plane trip was an event people talked about in those days, and so I settled down to enjoy myself. And I did—until we got to Nebraska. The plane touched down in Omaha, and the stewardess brought me a newspaper. I unfolded it, and the front page damn near leaped up and slapped me. BANK BANDITS CAPTURED, the headline read. KILLERS CAUGHT QUICKLY. A picture went with the story, a great big blowup of Lawrence Devol.

Devol had crashed a party in St. Paul and had stirred up so much trouble that the host had called the police. He must have been plastered, I thought to myself. When the cops got there, Devol proceeded to pile into them, and after a terrific struggle they locked him up downtown. When they searched his apartment, they found his share of the loot from the Minneapolis bank job. They also found an address book and staked out a house mentioned in the book. Three guys got nailed there, so the news story went, all armed with forty-five automatics, the same as our guys often carried. The paper didn't name the three, and I was worried. Maybe the three guys included Freddie or Doc. I hadn't heard from them since we separated at the apartment back in St. Paul.

The plane took off from Omaha, and once again the motion of the flight relaxed me. I fell asleep. I didn't wake until we were on the ground in Cheyenne, Wyoming, and as soon as I opened my eyes, I knew something was wrong. My 380 was gone. I couldn't find it on the seat or on the floor. I had to change planes at Cheyenne, and I walked into the airport expecting the worst kind of trouble.

I was trying to figure my next move when another passenger came up to me, a smooth-looking guy who'd been sitting behind me.

"Did you lose something on the plane?" he asked.

"Yeah, I did," I said. There was no point in fooling around. "I lost a 380 automatic."

"Come with me," he said.

We walked into the washroom.

"I felt something hit my foot," he said. He opened his briefcase and handed me my gun. "I don't know why you need a gun, but if you're ever in Los Angeles, you might want to look me up."

He held out his card. He was a criminal lawyer.

"Yeah," I said. "I won't forget you."

The trip was turning into a nightmare. My connecting flight to Reno was grounded and I had to stay over in Cheyenne. Next day I caught a plane west and got as far as Salt Lake City. The only plane operating between there and Reno at the time was a mail plane. I told them to book me on it and, Jesus, it turned out to be an open cockpit job. They put me in a tiny compartment in the nose with a couple of blankets. I wanted a parachute like the pilot.

"You don't need a parachute," an attendant said.

"If I don't need one, why does the pilot have one?"

They talked about regulations and never did give me an answer. Anyway, when we finally landed in Reno, there were no cabs, so I walked to the terminal building to use a phone.

"Don't go in there, sir," some guy yelled excitedly.

"What the hell are you talking about?" I asked.

"We're having an earthquake," he said.

That didn't even send a ripple through me.

"You know something?" I said. "An earthquake's the least of my goddamn troubles. I'm going to call a cab."

I ordered the driver to take me to the Rex, a club I knew in downtown Reno. And there in the back room they all were: Freddie, Doc, Bill Weaver, and Jess Doyle. None of them had heard about Devol's trouble until I broke the news. None of us, as it developed, was able to solve the mystery of the three arrested men until some weeks later when some guys drifted into Reno from the Midwest and told us that they were Devol's crazy brother Clarence, the one who used to pull the lovers' lane stickups, and a couple of other guys we'd never heard of. None of them, of course, had been even slightly involved in the Minneapolis bank job.

In Reno we felt a million miles away from Minneapolis and all its problems. Freddie, Ma and I rented a furnished house and settled down for a couple of months. We played keno at the clubs, went to the movies, sat around the Rex, and generally killed time. Whores were legal in Nevada and they were a diversion. On Christmas Day, we whipped up a nice party and, for a little change of pace, I made a side trip after New Year's to San Francisco.

Reno was quiet as far as action was concerned, but there were plenty of people in our line of business around taking it easy, and there was a lot of socializing. I met one kid whose company I enjoyed, a sharp young guy with a teen-ager's face and good taste in clothes. He was Lester Gillis, who would one day be the notorious Baby Face Nelson. He was an escapee out of Illinois and the Nevada boys were taking care of him. I used to go out to his place and have meals with him and his wife and two children. They were a pleasant family.

"He was Lester Gillis, who would one day be the notorious Baby Face Nelson. I used to go out to his place and have meals with him and his wife and two children. They were a pleasant family."
— UPI

Nelson had moved around a lot. He had been doing a bit in the Illinois State Penitentiary for a bank job when the authorities, not willing to let well enough alone, decided to prosecute him on yet another bank score. They were sore because he wouldn't testify against some other guys being tried on the same beef. Anyway, every day they took him by train from the joint in Joliet to a nearby town where the trial was being held, and every night they returned him to prison. One day on the train, Nelson asked to go to the toilet, and there he picked up a pistol that had been planted for him. When the train reached Joliet, Nelson and his guard got off and got into a cab. Nelson soon commandeered the taxi and ordered the driver to go out to the cemetery. There he handcuffed both the driver and the guard to a picket fence and made off in the car.

Two hoods, Three Finger Jack White and Klondike O'Donnell, agreed to help Nelson find a hiding place. They sent him to a San Francisco friend named Joe Pirrenti, who was the biggest rum runner on the Coast at that time. Nelson brought his family out and they settled in Sausalito, across the bay from San Francisco. Everything went along smoothly until his picture appeared in *True Detective Story*. People recognized him and he decided it was time to fly the coop. Pirrenti sent the Nelsons to Bill Graham and Jim McKay in Reno, the guys who paved the way for legalized gambling in Nevada.

Baby Face Nelson had some bullet-punctured years ahead of him, but at this point he was more or less being looked after financially by Graham and McKay and not liking it very much. He hated being dependent on the whims of these two guys. That was the rub. Anyway, the upshot of our many conversations was that once I returned East, I would see what I could do for him. We had all the men we could handle, but I figured maybe some other outfit could use him. Finally, in 1933, I did get him into an outfit in St. Paul.

" 'Goddamn Texas screwballs.' I asked him who the crazy couple was. 'Clyde Barrow and his girlfriend, Bonnie Parker . . . and sure as hell they're going to be shooting up drugstores and every other damn thing around here.' " — UPI

Nelson and I hadn't known each other as kids, but when we found out we had lived in the same neighborhood in Chicago, we developed a kind of bond. We had both hung out around West Division and Sacramento and even knew the same kids. We saw each other a lot.

The last time I saw Nelson in Reno, he was rubbing his fingertips with some powerful solution. A hood had told him the stuff would remove fingerprints. But from what I could see it was just raising blisters. His fingers were always paining him. But worse than the pain was the restlessness. Nelson wanted out of Reno. He wanted to get to work, sticking people up.

So did I, and by the middle of February, 1933, Freddie and I decided it was clear to return to the Midwest. We'd already made up our minds about our next score. It was to be a bank in Fairbury, Nebraska, and our base of operations would be Kansas City. We would set out from there for Fairbury and run the roads out of Fairbury back to Kansas City.

I flew down to Kansas City to set up the job. I had two objectives—to find an apartment for us in a quiet part of town and to line up Vern Miller for the job. I located the right apartment, but Miller, who'd driven so beautifully in the Minneapolis score, turned me down. He was busy, he said. He and some others were out to knock off an operator from the Burns Detective Agency who'd been assigned to break up a local jewelry-heisting ring.

I was disappointed, but I drove down to Joplin, Missouri, and ran into a funny situation when I went around to call on an old friend named Herb Farmer. Farmer was a congenial guy, and I was surprised when he seemed reluctant to invite me into his house. There were already three people sitting in the living room, a couple I didn't recognize and Mickey Carey, a character I knew, a guy who'd done a lot of time in Leavenworth on a narcotics charge. As for the couple, they looked like sharecroppers. He had a young face, a short fellow with light brown hair. She was a tiny thing, not more than one hundred pounds soaking wet, I imagined, and she had awfully squinty eyes. Both of their faces wore blank expressions, like many of the people you saw sitting on front steps in the rural parts of Texas and Oklahoma.

"These people here," Carey said, nodding at the couple, "have some Browning automatic rifles, and they want to know if somebody'd like to buy them."

"What would anybody want with those damn things?" I said.

"They're great if you want to jump out of a car and start fighting," Carey said. The couple didn't say a word. They just kept staring at me.

"Well, I suppose they're useful if you're caught in a building," I said. "But if you try running with one of them in your hands, well, you're likely to shoot yourself all to hell."

The couple stared some more, right through me, it seemed. Then Carey announced they were leaving, and all three of them filed out.

"Goddamn Texas screwballs," Farmer said after they'd pulled away in their car.

I asked him who the crazy couple was.

"Clyde Barrow and his girlfriend, Bonnie Parker. They've rented a house in Joplin, and sure as hell they're going to be shooting up drugstores and every other damn thing around here. I don't like it."

I'd heard about Bonnie and Clyde and none of it had been good. Barrow was a product of Southern chain gang prison camps and was wanted for killing cops all over the Southwest.

One thing was sure: Whenever Barrow and his girlfriend showed up someplace, trouble wasn't far behind.

In Joplin Bonnie and Clyde moved in with Clyde's brother Buck and his wife, Blanche. Their stay was a short one. They were jumped by the cops soon after they moved in and there was one hell of a shoot-out there. Cops were mowed down right and left. The four made good their escape but later, in Iowa, Buck was killed and Blanche captured. Bonnie and Clyde again escaped but on May 23, 1934, were shot to pieces in Louisiana by law enforcement officers led by former Texas Ranger Frank Hamer.

Even without Miller, the plans for the Fairbury caper moved along smoothly. We knew there were a few risks, and we made our preparations against them. We knew, for one thing, that the bank was the only one in town and that, therefore, the local cops would be ready to defend it as soon as something was up. We were also aware that the store owners in Fairbury were an aggressive bunch. They all knew sooner or later somebody would try to take the bank. They packed guns in their places and were always on the lookout for holdup men. The druggist was the principal vigilante and his store looked straight across the courthouse square to the bank.

To guard ourselves against all that opposition, we took in seven experienced men for the job: Freddie, Doc, me, Jess Doyle, Earl Christman, who had gone on the Concordia job and a few after it, and a pair of stickup guys from Chicago, Frank Nash and Volney Davis. All of us were armed to the teeth. We took along three machine guns, three rifles, half a dozen pistols, and several rounds of extra ammunition. And, in case of serious trouble, we threw a medicine kit full of quarter-grain phials of morphine into the car. We weren't fooling around on the Fairbury job.

We picked a warm sunny day in April and drove into town in the morning. We chose the hour carefully. The bank faced east, looking into the early morning sun, and to avoid glare the employees always kept the Venetian blinds pulled until noon. That suited us fine. With the blinds down, nobody could spot us from the sidewalk outside.

I liked the look of things: the bright day, the sleepy town, the drawn blinds. I felt confident as we pulled up. We split up into pairs, as usual, and walked toward the bank from different directions. Doyle stayed with the car. Freddie and Earl Christman made one pair. Doc and Volney Davis went together, and I ambled along with Frank Nash. We made it to the door of the bank and barged right on in as if we owned it.

"Bank robbers! Bank robbers!"

Some crazy woman on the street was shooting her mouth off. She hadn't seen the guns. We hadn't even gone into action. She just spotted us—strangers, I suppose—and opened up her mouth. We pushed into the bank, and the first sight that hit my eyes was a laughing teller. He thought we were joking or something. I slapped him across the face, hard, with my gun. Nobody was kidding around.

Freddie and I kept our guns up. We covered the tellers and customers, while the others scooped the money out of the cages. But it was tough concentrating. There was too much commotion out on the street. We could hear a dozen people yelling and hollering the same word:

"Robbers!"

I was worried about Doyle and the car. If we lost him and the car, we were marooned, sitting ducks for all those gun-happy merchants. I improvised a bit of defensive strategy. I told Nash, who was carrying one of the machine guns, to take up a position at the door where he could see on a direct line to the courthouse. If any cops or sheriff's men showed their noses, he was to open fire. He was also to cover me. I was going outside to back up Doyle.

When I hit the street, I got a temporary shock. Doyle wasn't in the car. Then I saw him. He was crouched beside the wall of the bank, holding a forty-five in each hand.

"The goddamn machine gun's jammed!" he shouted.

I ducked over to the car. The machine gun was sitting on

the front seat and it had a hundred-shot drum. I picked it up and tested its action.

"Hey, look!" Doyle screamed. "Look! Up the street!"

I glanced up. Men filled the end of the street from one side to the other. They were crouched down, moving slowly toward us, and they were carrying rifles. They started shooting. Bullets ricocheted off the pavement and the bank wall. I turned my attention to the machine gun. The damn thing *had* to work. I slipped a slug into the barrel and ejected it. The gun seemed okay.

Then, all of a sudden, it started spewing bullets all over the place. I'd triggered it off. It was jammed. It was aimed directly across the street and, with me still holding onto it, tight as I could, its stream of bullets sliced every which way across a brick wall and into a jewelry store. The store's glass window disintegrated in a split second, and glass and jewels and watches flew into the air and floated down onto the street. I swung left, and the path of bullets cut into the drug-store, sending up another shower of glass, wood, and cardboard.

The gun ran through the whole drum and then quit. I jammed a new fifty-shot drum into it and flipped it over to Doyle. Meanwhile, the vigilantes down the street had ducked into doorways, frightened, at least for the moment, by my display of gunmanship. The new trouble was coming from the courthouse. The cops had loaded their rifles and were peppering the bank from their cover. Nash was supposed to handle them, but now he was having trouble with *his* machine gun.

I dashed back into the bank.

"What the hell's wrong with you?" I yelled into his face.

"I didn't load the damn thing the right way!"

I fixed his gun in a couple of seconds flat, and Nash opened up on the courthouse.

Christman and Doc were covering four people just inside

the bank door. They were hostages. Each guy intended to use two hostages as cover to reach the car. Christman went first. His hostages were men, and the three of them ducked out of the bank door. I turned my attention to the courthouse. A guy ran out of it with a Luger in his hand. From behind me, somebody, probably Freddie, opened up with a rifle. He shot four or five times, and on the last shot, he dropped the guy.

I looked back to the sidewalk to check on Christman. I couldn't believe what I saw. He had his machine gun pointed into the belly of one of his hostages and he was pouring shots into him.

I ran over to him.

"Jesus!" I screamed. "What's going on?"

"These sons of bitches!" Christman shouted. I could see he was in pain. "The two of them separated so somebody could take a clear shot at me! I'm hit! Through the back!"

I dragged him into the back seat of the car and hollered for the rest of the guys to get the hell out of the bank. Guns were still cracking from the direction of the courthouse and from doorways down the street. Christman's two hostages were lying flat out on the sidewalk. Blood was dripping all over the place. Broken glass and empty shell cases were decorating the landscape.

Doyle jumped in behind the wheel. Freddie, Doc, Nash, and Davis hustled out of the bank. They pushed the two girls in front of them. Gunfire from the courthouse stopped. We stationed one girl on the left running board and the other on the right. And we pulled away.

For good measure, I stuck my forty-five out the window and threw a few shots down the street.

We'd run the roads a dozen times and we drove like hell. If there was a tail on us, we shook it. After ten miles we let the girls out, and further on we stopped to check Christman's wound. A bullet had passed through his collarbone and I could make out tiny splinters of bone where the shot had gone into him. I jabbed some morphine into him and washed out the blood with some drugstore prescription whiskey.

We zigzagged across Nebraska and into Kansas. We steered clear of main roads, stopping only to pick up gasoline at prearranged drops and to shoot some more morphine into Christman. We kept going and reached Kansas City without seeing a single cop.

The job was finished except for the loose ends, like tending to Christman. Vern Miller rounded up a doctor who pronounced him in pretty good shape and shipped him off to a place in the country to recuperate. Before Christman left, we counted up the loot and, despite the gunplay and pressure and rush, we still came away with $37,000 in cash and another $39,000 in World War I Liberty Bonds.

There was one other loose end. We had to check on the damage we'd left behind in Fairbury. We looked through the papers. Fairbury wasn't front page news to Kansas City, but we found the story of the robbery inside. I was amazed—in all that shooting nobody had been killed. The guy who took the shots point blank in the stomach from Christman survived. So did the guy who ran out of the courthouse firing the Luger. They all survived. There were eight of them—all in the hospital, all with wounds, but all still alive. I couldn't believe it.

6

"Ma Was Always Somebody in Our Lives"

THE MOST RIDICULOUS story in the annals of crime is that Ma Barker was the mastermind behind the Karpis-Barker Gang.

I must have read in a couple of hundred newspapers and magazines that it was she who trained her sons and the rest of us in the finer points of thieving, kidnapping, bank robbing, and murder. The articles I've read are always going on about the "crime school" she ran in Tulsa, Oklahoma. Ma Barker never ran a crime school in Tulsa or any other place. As a matter of fact, the legend of Ma Barker, whose full name was Arizona Clark Barker, only grew up years after her death and only then in order to justify the manner in which she met her death at the hands of the FBI.

If you believe the legends, Ma was the most famous and

the most feared woman in the United States at one time, a thief and a killer. Ma was none of these things. She wasn't a leader of criminals or even a criminal herself. The proof is that in her entire life, she was never once mugged or printed by the police. There is not one official police photograph of her in existence or a set of fingerprints taken while she was alive. If she had been such a menace to society, the police would surely have had her mug shot and prints on file. I challenge the FBI to prove otherwise.

It's probably too late to rewrite the legend, but I'd like to try.

The idea that Ma was the brains behind our five years of holdups and crimes is strongly entrenched in North America. In books, kids' comics, detective fiction, and movies and, for that matter, in every other entertainment outlet Ma has been described as a genius of crime for so long that nobody will ever believe that she was to us, in the Karpis-Barker Gang, a simple woman and the mother of Freddie and Doc.

Ma was always *somebody* in our lives. Love didn't enter into it really. She was somebody we looked after and took with us when we moved from city to city, hideout to hideout.

It's no insult to Ma's memory that she just didn't have the brains or know-how to direct us on a robbery. It wouldn't have occurred to her to get involved in our business, and we always made a point of only discussing our scores when Ma wasn't around. We'd leave her at home when we were arranging a job, or we'd send her to a movie. Ma saw a lot of movies.

You only had to spend a few hours with Ma to see she wasn't the criminal type. She was just an old-fashioned homebody from the Ozarks. I never understood why her sons turned out to be major-league criminals. Ma wasn't, and she brought the Barker boys up. She was a simple woman. Her spare time was spent working jigsaw puzzles and listening to the radio— the way any mother would whose family had grown up.

Ma was superstitious, gullible, simple, cantankerous and, well, generally law-abiding. She wasn't suited for a role in the Karpis-Barker Gang.

I would never deny that Ma was completely ignorant of what Freddie, Doc, and I and the others were up to. She knew we were criminals and that we'd spent time in prison. But she was never informed of the specifics. She was, after all, a woman from the Ozarks and had no sophistication and no background that would make her want to know more about how we earned our money. She never read newspapers or looked at magazines and, as Freddie was always pointing out, the only radio stations she tuned into were the hillbilly stations, the ones that didn't bother with news. Ma wasn't stupid. She knew the reason we were constantly on the move and switching apartments had something to do with avoiding the police. But she was naïve and uninformed and didn't concern herself with the younger generation's problems.

Our meeting came in the late spring of 1931, shortly after I left Lansing. In prison Freddie had given me Ma's address, as we planned to join forces after our sentences, and since he'd been sprung before me, he told me that I could pick up an address for him from his mother in Tulsa. I followed his advice. But first I called on Carol Hamilton, whom I'd already met in Tulsa and who was Herman Barker's widow and, therefore, Ma Barker's daughter-in-law. Carol directed me out to Ma's house on Archer Avenue. It sat in a field of weeds on the north side of the railroad tracks with what appeared to be a tarpaulin for a roof.

As I approached, I saw this little dumpy old woman standing on a box, wearing a pair of bib overalls over a man's sweater. It was hard to tell how tall she was. It looked as though she had ringlets in her hair, but when I got closer it just looked stringy.

Anyway, she was trying to drive a nail into the frame of a window screen and she could hardly reach it. I was close enough now to see she was about five feet two inches tall, and hefty. Maybe 140 pounds. And she wore gold-rimmed glasses. She hadn't heard me come up and when I said, "Excuse me," she damn near fell off that box, she was so startled.

"Are you Mrs. Barker?" I asked.

"I sure am," she replied. She sounded like a real little Ozark hillbilly.

"I want to get hold of Freddie," I went on.

"Who are you?"

"I'm the guy who celled with Freddie in Lansing."

"Oh, yeah, he told me about you. He told me you'd be getting out soon. He came down to visit me when he got out. He's a real good boy."

I gave her a rundown on what I had done and when I told her about going to Carol's place, she exploded. "That hussy," she said. "What were you doing over there?" But when I asked if there was something wrong, she just changed the subject.

She agreed to send a telegram to Freddie and I gave her a dollar. Then she asked me to hold the screen while she hammered the nail in. I told her I'd look after it and to get down off the box.

"My man ain't here right now," she said. "I thought I'd put the screen up because the flies are getting bad."

I followed her into the house and, Jesus, what a place. There was no bathroom, just an outhouse. There was an old washtub on the porch. The table had oilcloth on it. There was no electricity. Just a lantern on a table and another on a rickety old dresser. There was an old sink with no taps. Under the sink there was a bucket.

"I'm going to get out of these overalls and go down to Western Union," she said. Then she told me to go back to Carol's and she would bring me the news from Freddie.

"Don't say a word to that hussy," she warned. "Don't tell

her what you're doing, or where you're going, or anything."

I thought at first that maybe Ma had a specific beef against Carol, but this wasn't so. It was just that Ma didn't like female competition. She wanted to be the only woman who counted with her boys. She sometimes tried to justify her feelings by telling us that in our positions, we shouldn't take up with women. We couldn't trust them, she'd say—they'd give us away to the police. But Ma's reasoning, in my opinion, was just an excuse to monopolize her boys.

Back at Carol's, I told about my visit. Ma didn't live with Freddie's father. Freddie had told me this. But she had referred to somebody as "my man." So, who was he? Carol knew about the guy and didn't feel the least bit charitable toward him.

"He's a worthless bastard," she said. "A guy named Arthur Dunlop. Too lazy to work and too scared to steal. They're just barely getting by. I buy them groceries now and then."

The next morning the buzzer rang and Ma came in. Freddie had telegraphed that he wanted me to take the train to Joplin, Missouri, that very day and that I would be met there.

I thanked Mrs. Barker and we shook hands. "You tell Freddie I said to be a good boy and come visit me as soon as he can," she said.

In time, I became one of Ma's "boys." She and I grew very close in the years that all of us—Freddie, Doc, Ma, and I, and various assorted friends and wives—lived together. I moved in with the Barkers shortly after that first meeting in Tulsa, and right from the start, Ma and I had a feeling for one another. Freddie used to say that Ma would rather be with me than with him. "You don't get on her nerves the way I do," Freddie would say.

Probably the real reason Ma liked me, or at least one of the reasons, was that I was always showing her a good time. We went to movies and carnivals, and once, when we were staying in Reno, I took her on a side trip to San Francisco.

We went by plane and she got a real bang out of it. Actually, she liked simple pleasures more than expensive treats. Bingo, for instance—Ma was nuts about bingo, and I took her to many games. Bingo bored me, but I didn't mind showing Ma a good time.

Ma was a good sport. She had to be to put up with our gypsy way of living. We'd move into a place, get comfortable, and then a couple of weeks or months later we'd say, "Ma, it's time to go." She wouldn't complain or question. In half an hour she'd have all her clothes and belongings gathered up. She wouldn't even ask where we were headed.

The toughest move for her was probably the very first one. It was from a farm near Thayer, Missouri, late in 1931. Freddie had rented the place. All his life, he said, he'd wanted to settle his mother into a pleasant home, and while the farm wasn't exactly a palace—it was quite small and had no running water—Ma liked it. She was prepared to spend the rest of her days there, but as things turned out, she didn't last more than a few weeks.

The end of life on the farm came suddenly early one Saturday morning. Freddie and Bill Weaver, who was also living in the area, borrowed my car to drive around and check out some possible jobs. They were gone for several hours, straight through the Saturday morning. When they returned to the farm they were driving Bill's old jalopy, not my car, and they warned us we'd better clear out of the district fast.

Freddie and Bill had killed a sheriff. They said they'd run into a couple of flat tires on the road. They pulled into a garage in West Plains, Missouri, and while they were sitting around waiting for the repairs, the local sheriff strolled over. That sheriff had a tough reputation. He'd knocked over more than a couple of holdup gangs single-handed. He was an old-style, two-fisted, quick-shooting Western sheriff, and he suspected that Freddie and Weaver were up to no good. He questioned them for a couple of minutes, didn't care for their answers, and then ordered them to stand up for a frisking.

Freddie wasn't going to wait for the sheriff to find his gun. He pulled it out and blasted him. He must have been a strong old buzzard because, even with a couple of bullets in him, he managed to draw his own pistol. But before he could squeeze the trigger, Weaver let him have it three times in the back.

"The hell of it was," Freddie said later, "that there was a bank across the street, and everybody in the damn town thought we were sticking it up. They came running down the street with their rifles and started firing. We got away, but we ran into a ditch and had to walk all the way over to Bill's place to pick up his jalopy. The thing is those people are going to find your car in the ditch and trace it down here."

We told Ma to pack up. She was unhappy about it and didn't understand why, but she cleaned out the house in quick time. She realized she was saying good-bye to her new farm. Freddie took her with him in the jalopy to our friend Herb Farmer's place in Joplin, Missouri, where I was to meet them later. In the meantime, I decided to stick around on my own to see if the cops would find our place. I walked to a wooded bluff and hid myself. Less than three hours later, I saw two sedans pull into the yard. Each car held four or five guys, carrying weapons.

That was enough for me. I walked cross country, staying in the woods as much as possible. I was a stranger in that part of the state and didn't recognize the roads or landmarks. I kept moving, and eventually I stumbled into a little town called Mammoth Spring in Arkansas, waited until dark, and then broke into the Ford agency. Soon, I was driving north in a brand-new Model A sedan, wearing one of those long white coats that garage attendants sometimes wore. The coat was a necessity because by now my clothes were a mess.

Just like Ma, I was saying good-bye to the farm and to rural Missouri. I liked life there as much as she did. But I was going to be haunted for years by the incident in West Plains. The people there had marked me as the killer of their sheriff. Freddie and Bill had done the job while I was miles away, but the local cops linked the car to me, and since there were no witnesses to the shooting, it was blamed on me. For years afterward, I was hunted as the murderer of the sheriff of West Plains.

All of our fast moves were complicated by the fact that Ma's boyfriend traveled with us. She'd been separated for years from her real husband, the father of the Barker boys, and she'd taken up with this Dunlop. She seemed to like him and let him live with her and sponge off her.

He *looked* presentable enough. He was a slim, gray-haired guy, about a head taller than Ma, who kept himself reasonably neat and tidy. But he was a pain in the ass. When I took Ma out to the movies, I'd have to take Dunlop along too. When we were buying food and clothes, we always had to remember to pick up a share for him. And Dunlop did nothing in return—didn't work, didn't go on scores, didn't help out around the house. He didn't even do a very good job of keeping Ma happy, which was the only reason we let him hang around.

As time wore on, Freddie and I began to realize that Dunlop had two really serious drawbacks. He was a drunk and an ingrate. Even though he owed every stitch of clothes and every bit of food to us, he'd never thank Freddie or me for anything. All we'd hear was whines. He didn't like moving from place to place and he didn't like being bossed by young punks. His complaints got so monotonous that Freddie grew to hate him, no matter what Ma thought. Freddie never called Dunlop by name. He would simply refer to him as "the old bastard."

Half the time "the old bastard" had his nose in a glass of bootleg booze. He was a real lush, and worse, he didn't know how to handle liquor. When he was loaded, he'd turn mean and abuse Ma. Ma put up with it, but I didn't have to. I'd tell him to shut his mouth and clear out until he was sober.

My worst fight with Dunlop happened the night I noticed he was packing a gun that Freddie and I had given him in a weak moment. It was a thirty-eight, and he had it sticking out of his right-hand pants' pocket. He'd been heckling Ma and me all that night. Finally, I lured him into the kitchen, promising him another drink. When we were out of Ma's hearing, I told him to let me have the thirty-eight. He told me to go to hell, and I blew up. I pulled out my own forty-five.

"Don't raise your voice, don't make a wrong move," I said. "Try either one and you're a dead son of a bitch. Just hand over the gun and shut up."

Dunlop obeyed but it was already too late for him. I didn't know it at the moment, but he had already made the mistake that was to finish him.

We were all living in St. Paul at the time. It was the winter of 1932, and Freddie and I had established good connections with various burglars and big shots. We'd moved into a furnished house in West St. Paul, and the woman who owned it had a son who ran a couple of speakeasies. The son liked to drink his own products, and he and Dunlop used to sit around getting tanked and shooting the breeze. This made Freddie and me nervous. Who could tell what old Dunlop might spill?

Well, I found out just how talkative he was sooner than I expected. The day after our skirmish in the kitchen, at eight in the morning, I took a phone call from Harry Sawyer, a St. Paul friend of mine who had contacts at police headquarters. Harry had bad news. It seemed that somebody had tipped off the cops about us. Pictures of Freddie and me had appeared in *True Detective Story* a couple of weeks earlier and, according to Sawyer, a police informant had gone to headquarters with the magazine and a load of information about us. Sawyer's man on the police force was stalling the raid against our house long enough to allow Harry to tip us off.

ˈ I knew damn well who the cops' informant was. It was the landlady's son. And I knew where he'd gotten his dope. Obviously, Dunlop had spilled everything during one of their drinking bouts. Dunlop was more stupid than malicious and probably was bragging when he let the landlady's son in on his secrets. Still, the damage was done, and I had to hustle Dunlop and Ma out of the house and take care of things by myself, since Freddie was away.

We cleared out in two minutes flat, and in the car, I faced Ma and Dunlop with the situation. Dunlop admitted he'd talked too much. He was too scared to lie, and he tried to excuse himself by saying he'd been drunk. I told him he was a rotten son of a bitch, and I took him to a hotel and checked him in under a phony name.

I wanted to talk to Ma alone. She was in a state of shock. I drove her to a friend's house, and we talked about Dunlop for a couple of hours. I said she'd be better off without him, and she agreed. Out of loyalty, she didn't want to criticize Dunlop, but I gathered she'd had her fill. I told Ma that she and I and Freddie should settle in Kansas City until the excitement in St. Paul cooled off. I promised I'd give Dunlop some cash and ship him off to Chicago. She went along with my ideas and seemed at ease.

Dunlop never reached Chicago, though. His body was found a couple of days later, floating facedown in a lake just across the Wisconsin state line. He had been shot three times in the back with a forty-five.

I didn't shoot Dunlop. Nor did Freddie. It was done by Jack Peifer. Peifer was a big name in various illegal operations around St. Paul, and he often hired Freddie and me to pull jobs for him. He knocked off Dunlop as a kind of return favor to us.

Life was more pleasant without Dunlop's drinking and

whining. Even Ma admitted that she didn't miss him, and for the next few years, Ma, Freddie, Doc, and I were a pretty contented family. She didn't live with us constantly. There were weeks and months when we had to leave her alone somewhere. When the cops were breathing hard, or when we had to carry out an important job, we'd stash Ma away in a safe location and leave her with plenty of cash.

Ma missed us when we were away and she showed her affection by treating us with extra-special care when we came back. She was always laying out spreads of fried chicken and mashed potatoes and that kind of biscuit the women of the Ozarks specialize in. Whenever she had a chance, she'd put on a party. When her son Doc arrived in the late summer of 1932, after sitting it out for thirteen years in McAlester, Ma threw a real bash. She didn't drink much, but on the occasion of Doc's coming-out party she knocked back a few of her special eggnogs laced with shots of rum.

Ma never objected when Freddie and I arrived with an unexpected guest. We were always taking in guys on the lam or ex-cons we'd chosen for specific jobs, and Ma would go right along with us. She'd make up a fresh bed and set another place at the dinner table. Her generosity, however, only applied to men. It was a rare time when she'd let us bring women to the house. And for most of the time we lived with her, whenever Freddie or I got serious about a girl, we'd move out of Ma's place and keep the girls in another hotel or apartment. It was a crazy system and often created friction with our women, who couldn't understand why we were so careful of the old lady's feelings. But Freddie and I preferred to avoid Ma's jealous anger.

Ma was an odd character in many other ways. For one thing she looked a little peculiar. It was sometimes hard for us not to laugh when we saw her propped up in one of our cars. She was so short that her head barely rose above the dashboard. She needed boosting up to see out, and we bought her an air cushion that she took everywhere. Riding along on her cushion, peeking out of one of the big, two-tone, twelve-cylinder Auburns we preferred in those days, Ma looked like a slightly nutty old queen.

The strange things she did to her hair didn't make her more glamorous. When she felt like dolling up, she'd turn her hair into a mass of curls. The style looked as if it belonged on a little girl, but Ma's sixty-year-old face spoiled the effect. The night I took her to the 1933 Chicago World's Fair, she performed a real job on herself. She piled on the curls for the evening. We visited all the exhibits that appealed to her, like the "Ripley's Believe It or Not" show and the Motordome, and she stuffed herself with cotton candy all night. Well, after a few hours, what with the curls and the dirt and the dust and her windblown clothes and her face covered with dried cotton candy, Ma looked like an exhibit out of the Ripley show herself.

With her personality, brains, and style, it was impossible for Ma Barker to become the mastermind of the Karpis-Barker Gang. Her participation in our careers was limited to one function. Whether she was aware of it or not, Ma made a nearly foolproof cover for Freddie and me and Doc. When we traveled together, we moved as a mother and three sons. What could look more innocent? We usually told our landlords and apartment house superintendents that we were salesmen, taking care of our widowed mother. The story never aroused anybody's suspicion. And the cops were always thrown off by our family appearance. They could never believe that fellows who were kind to their mother could ever be members of a dangerous gang of criminals. They were wrong, of course. As wrong as the people who started the legend that Ma Barker was the brains of the gang.

7

"Everybody Had a Price"

SOMETIMES I USED to think in the early 1930's that you could bribe the President of the United States. All you needed was enough money. I didn't mean any particular insult to Herbert Hoover or to Franklin D. Roosevelt. I just meant that everybody in those days seemed to have his price. You could bribe any kind of official, from a jail guard to a mayor or a governor. I saw enough evidence in my time of the power of money over morals to believe that anything was possible if you could come up with the cash. Everybody had a hand out, and corruption was just as obvious in high places as it was in low.

The matter of getting out of jail was a perfect example of the way the system functioned. It was the same as in everything else—cough up the money to the right parties and the chances were pretty favorable that you could avoid prison no matter how strong a case the cops had against you. The size of the bribe depended on the importance of the town or city you were arrested in. You could often buy your way out of a jail in many of the two-bit Midwest towns with a comparatively small payoff to the jailer or the sheriff. But in a big city prison, the dealing was more complicated and you usually needed to raise enough cash to bribe four or five officials up and down the line.

My old pal Lawrence Devol once got himself sprung for a mere $50 dropped into a jailer's pocket. It was in the winter of 1930 in a little Oklahoma town called Ponca City after he'd been nabbed on a burglary charge. But, by contrast, a couple of years later, it took a $1,500 bribe to spring Volney Davis from McAlester. Davis was a close friend of Doc Barker and Doc insisted that we arrange to get his pal released on parole. Davis had served thirteen years of his life term, and we contacted a big operator in St. Paul who said he could arrange an early parole for $1,500. We asked no questions, and on payment the big operator delivered. None of us knew what officials were paid off, and we didn't ask. It was probably best not to.

I knew a State Senator in Oklahoma who wasn't at all shy about the fact that money could buy him. Everybody in the burglary business or in holdups, in fact anyone who made his living on the shady side of the law, knew that the Senator in question could swing the state parole board any way he was paid to swing it, and on one occasion, in the summer of 1935, I decided to try his services.

I was planning a payroll train job at the time, and I needed the help of a good, strong stickup man, someone like Sam Coker, who just happened to be residing in McAlester Penitentiary. Coker was eligible for parole a few months later, but I couldn't wait to get on with the job, and I sent a contact man, a fellow named Burrhead Keady, to see the crooked Senator. Burrhead brought word back to me: The Senator would guarantee immediate release for a payment of $1,000.

Burrhead took the money to the Senator's office and the Senator, who was a sport, invited Burrhead to have a drink. Well, one thing led to another, and in no time, Burrhead was betting the Senator a new Stetson that he couldn't get Coker's release papers signed within twenty-four hours. The Senator took him up, and the upshot was that at one o'clock in the morning, the Senator and Burrhead, both of them heavily into the sauce, were pounding on the front door of McAlester demanding to talk to a prison official.

You had to hand it to the Senator—he knew how to throw his weight around. He pointed out to the official, who'd been roused out of his sleep, that he was a member of the State Senate and that unless the official obliged him, he'd take a close look at the year's appropriations for prisons. The official ordered the guards to wake Sam Coker and to dig out a new suit for him to wear on his trip out of prison. The Senator thanked the official, and just to show there were no hard feelings, he invited him to join them in a little drink out of the whiskey bottle they'd thoughtfully brought along. The three of them sat down at a table in the prison kitchen, and when Coker arrived, he sat down, too, and everyone drank to Sam's new freedom.

The only trouble with the custom of bribes and payoffs as far as I was concerned was that I learned about it too late. If I'd understood it sooner, I could have saved myself the beating I took in Kansas City. A few days before the police arrested Devol and me, we'd been tipped off by a pal to tell the cops, if we were in trouble, that we were friends of someone named Martinelli. Sure enough, right after we reached headquarters, the chief of police, a guy named Doyle, walked in and looked us over.

"You fellows know anyone in Kansas City?" he asked.

"What do you mean know anyone?" I answered, playing dumb. "We just got in here today."

"Never mind the crap," the chief said. "I'm asking you guys now before something happens to you. Do you know anyone in Kansas City? Do you know Martinelli?"

I really played dumb. Maybe I was too naïve. Maybe I was too much of a tough punk. Maybe I just didn't believe in the magic power of this mysterious Martinelli. Anyway, I said that I didn't know a soul in Kansas City. The chief left, and the rest of the cops proceeded to bust in my face.

The next day the cops said, "Why the hell didn't you tell us you knew Martinelli? You could have walked out of this place free and clear, you stupid bastard."

By then it was too late. The cops already knew that I was an escapee from Hutchinson and had to be returned. But, just for my own information, they told me that Martinelli was a city politician who represented a large ward of Italians. Martinelli delivered the Italian vote in every election, and he did a lot of favors for crooks and burglars, like the guy who tipped me off about him, who lived in his ward. One word from Martinelli and the cops would have sprung Devol and me. It was a tough lesson, but at least I realized that from then on, no matter what city I was in, I should check out the name of the local Martinelli.

A year after the Kansas City incident, after I'd served my time in Hutchinson and Lansing and been released, I did manage to act smart in a situation where I could have found myself locked up for a couple of years. The cops had arrested Freddie Barker and me for a jewelry store job we pulled in Henryetta, Oklahoma. They transferred Freddie to Claremore, where there were charges against him, and he escaped in record time. They took me to Okmulgee, the county seat, and I settled down to wait for the worst.

As the days went by, the jailer and I became pretty friendly. I realized he was feeling me out about something, and one morning he sprung it on me. He said if I could return some of the stolen jewelry, I could probably make a deal. In no time at all, it was agreed among the jailer, me, a lawyer in town who acted as a kind of intermediary and the jewelry store owner, whose name was Black that if I coughed up $100 for legal fees and returned most of the stolen merchandise, I'd get off with a suspended sentence. I wired my sister Emily in Chicago for the $100, and I instructed a girlfriend of mine to bring the jewels into court in a fruit jar where I'd hidden them.

The trial was called, and it went off as smooth as glass. Black, the jeweler, took the fruit jar into an anteroom and satisfied himself that most of the stolen stuff was there. He told the judge that he didn't want to testify in any charge against me, and the judge, who'd already been coached by the lawyer, gave me a three-year suspended sentence. To cap the day's proceedings, the lawyer, the judge, the jeweler, my girlfriend and I all drove over to the jewelry store, the one that Freddie and I had broken into, and toasted our deal with some glasses of illegal home brew.

There were all kinds of arrangements to be made with people willing to go on the take. Some were just plain crooked cops. There was a detective in Oklahoma for instance, who considered detection a sideline to grafting and wheeling and dealing. He operated in Tulsa and, one time in 1931, he broke in on Freddie and me, not to arrest us, but to set us up for a job in a downtown jewelry store called Goldberg's. The detective said he and another cop would cover for us in a marked police car. Freddie and I turned the deal down, and a couple of weeks later who arrested us in Tulsa for the jewelry burglary in Henryetta? It was the detective, getting his own back.

I met cops all over the Midwest who were just as much criminals as I was. I even had a friend, a guy I used to take with me on holdups, who was an ex-cop. His name was Phil Courtney, one of the members of the gang when we took the Northwestern Bank in Minneapolis, and earlier in his career he'd worked as a motorcycle cop in Cicero, Illinois. Al Capone got him the job, and Phil's duty was to follow Capone's beer trucks on deliveries and scare off hijackers.

Some of the cops and officials were damn clever about the deals they set up. The sheriff in Miami, Oklahoma, for instance, had an almost foolproof scheme he used to work with a lawyer who practiced in that part of the state. There were plenty of crooks and burglars hanging out around Miami in the early 1930's, and when one of them was arrested in another town, no matter what the charge was, the arresting police would receive a flyer from Miami pointing out that the man was wanted back in Miami. The flyer would emphasize that Miami was offering a $250 or $300 reward, and, since the cops could always use a little extra reward money, they'd invariably ship the man to Miami. The flyer was, of course, a phony, and the Miami sheriff would promptly release the prisoner to the custody of his lawyer friend, who would, in turn, collect a tidy fee of $1,200 to $1,500 from the freed prisoner. And the two of them, sheriff and lawyer, after paying the reward money, would split an easy profit.

Lawyers, I found, were often useful middlemen when we wanted something crooked pulled around a courthouse. They might not have been too useful at handling themselves in court—at least many of the shysters who worked for me didn't show much savvy—but many of them seemed to know how to work a payoff or how to come up with a valuable piece of information. They were particularly handy for smuggling equipment, notes, and drugs into guys behind bars. Different lawyers I met had different techniques. Some handled the job themselves, pretending to be calling on the prisoner for consultation. Some worked through guards and jailers, guys they paid off. But no matter how they handled it, they always demanded high fees. I met an old member of the John Dillinger Gang at one time who told me he'd paid a Chicago lawyer $5,000 to get a gun into Dillinger himself when he was in jail at Crown Point, Indiana.

I paid the same amount to a lawyer from Kansas City as a fee to put a forty-five automatic in Harvey Bailey's hands. Bailey was a partner of mine on several stickups, and he was waiting trial in jail at Fort Scott, Kansas, on a bank robbery charge. Part of the $5,000 deal with the lawyer was to pay off somebody connected with the court to let Bailey off. The lawyer failed on that end of the deal—Bailey drew a ten-to-fifty-year sentence—but I knew he came through on the gun smuggling arrangement, because shortly after Bailey started serving his time in Lansing, the jailers shook down his old cell in the jail and found a forty-five.

Corruption wasn't always just a case of one crooked lawyer in town or a few cops on the take. Sometimes, it was a whole town or a whole city administration that was corrupt. Criminals used to talk about "safe cities." They were places where the fix was in from top to bottom, and guys like me could relax. The chances were slim that in those cities we'd ever get arrested. And there were plenty of towns in the Midwest where, absolutely, the fix was in.

Cleveland, for instance, was a good town for criminals. In fact, at one point in 1936 the FBI gave out the news that a few months earlier they had me lined up for capture in Cleveland but that someone in the local district attorney's office had tipped me off in time to avoid the FBI trap. I never got cozy with the Cleveland cops or civic officials, but in the few months I was there I lined up one valuable connection. He was a guy named Frank Noonan, who owned a private detective agency and had once been in the slot-machine racket. Anyway, he had a very good friend with whom he had gone to school and who was now no less than the Assistant Attorney General of the United States. His name was Joe Keenan and he had been the prosecutor in the Urschel and Touhy kid-nappings.

Well, Noonan decided he'd take us out to dinner, and it tickled his sense of humor to think of the Assistant Attorney General discussing crime with a guy who had become one of the country's top criminals.

Noonan introduced me as a gambler and Keenan took this all in without batting an eye. Noonan kept pouring drinks into this guy, and before long he was half swacked and very talkative. One of his favorite topics of conversation was how he had settled Harvey Bailey when everybody from Hoover on down knew that Bailey wasn't guilty.

Keenan was proud of how he had fixed Bailey. Bailey had robbed banks and lammed out of that joint in Kansas and owed a lot of years. It didn't matter in Keenan's view that Bailey was innocent of the charge on which he was convicted.

"What does it matter where he's doing his time?" he asked.

Keenan, bombed, gave me lots of useful information. For instance, he'd drop newsy items like how many FBI agents were in town and what tactics they were using.

The fix was really in in Cleveland. Gambling could never survive without political cooperation and in the Cleveland area it was going night and day on a terrific scale. The main center was a place called the Harvard Club in Newburg Heights, a village completely surrounded by the city of Cleveland. The club was located in an old walkathon hall, and it had enough room to accommodate every crap table in the entire city of Reno. There were slot machines, crap tables, roulette wheels, and on the first night I visited the place, there must have been a crowd of at least 1,500 people, all anxious to throw away their money. And they were doing it with the blessing of a few cops and politicans who drew their own share of the house take.

Hot Springs, Arkansas, was another comfortable town for criminals. Many crooks chose it for their vacations. They went there for the springs and the mud baths, and they could be absolutely certain that no cop, from the chief on down, would lay a finger on them. All the local people asked was that you spent your money in their stores and hotels and bars and restaurants, and guys like Lucky Luciano, who was a frequent visitor, always spread around their cash in bills of large denominations. As a matter of fact, it was Luciano himself who provided a prize example of how openly cooperative with criminals the Hot Springs police were. When Tom Dewey, the New York City district attorney, wanted to extradite Luciano from Arkansas, he appealed direct to the state police to arrest Lucky. Dewey knew it was useless to send in the Hot Springs city police to do the job. They'd just refuse—or else they'd tip Lucky off.

But, of all the Midwest cities, the one that I knew best was St. Paul, and it was a crooks' haven. Every criminal of any importance in the 1930's made his home at one time or another in St. Paul. If you were looking for a guy you hadn't seen for a few months, you usually thought of two places— prison or St. Paul. If he wasn't locked up in one, he was probably hanging out in the other. St. Paul was a good spot for both pleasure and business. You could relax in its joints and speakeasies without any fear of arrest, and when you were planning a score, you could have your pick of all the top men at all the top crimes.

I didn't ever deal directly with the police and politicians who made St. Paul so congenial. I didn't have to. I was friendly with the middlemen, the guys who handled payoffs and negotiated relations between the crooks and the city, and I left it to them to pass the word and the money back and forth. The two most important guys I knew were Harry Sawyer and Jack Peifer, and they swung a lot of weight.

Sawyer and Peifer were in some ways rivals. They had similar contacts at city hall and police headquarters, and they had the same interest in beating people out of their money.

But they operated differently. Peifer was involved in the rackets and Sawyer wasn't. Ordinary crooks in those days were guys who pulled jobs at random, bank stickups, burglaries, heists of different kinds. Rackets guys, on the other hand, were organized and monopolized activities like prostitution, drug traffic, bookmaking, and rum running. Peifer tended more to rackets operations, while Sawyer was a freelance boss, but both of them cooperated in keeping St. Paul safe for stickup men like me.

Peifer owned a club called the Hollyhocks. It was a glamor spot, and Peifer used it as his headquarters for running the slot machine business and his other interests. I preferred Harry Sawyer's club. It was called the Green Lantern and used a cigar store as a front on Wabasha Avenue. Out back it was set up with booths where you could order the best beer in town—in fact the only beer that, in those Prohibition days, hadn't had the alcohol taken out of it at the breweries.

Sawyer ran the Green Lantern like a host at a great party, and I liked the way he handled himself. He certainly did all kinds of favors for the Karpis-Barker Gang. Sawyer was the guy who tipped us off about the raid from the cops after old Dunlop blew the whistle on us. Sawyer also passed on the word when the Minnesota Bureau of Apprehension wanted us to go easy on our cigarette thefts. That was the time we'd gone in heavily for stealing cigarettes, and the bureau told Sawyer to warn us that unless we stopped it would post an armed guard in every wholesale cigarette spot in the state. We appreciated the advice and got out of the cigarette business. We appreciated, too, Sawyer's role as our personal banker. Whenever we scored on a bank job, we would put a chunk of the money in Sawyer's hands for our savings. We knew from experience that it was safer with him than it would have been in a regular bank.

The Green Lantern was always my personal headquarters

in St. Paul. I knew everyone in the place, and if I didn't Sawyer would introduce me. Everybody had the same things in common—stealing, killing, and looting. Everybody had traveled to the same places—McAlester, Hutchinson, and Lansing. It was every day of the week, like a perpetual party.

The greatest blowout Sawyer threw in the place, in my experience was on New Year's Eve, 1932. If the cops had decided to grab everybody who went in and out of the Green Lantern that night, there would have been no crime spree of 1932 and 1933. Most of the guys greeted the arrival of 1932 with Sawyer's booze, but I didn't drink. I ate Sawyer's hard-boiled eggs and sent out to McCormick's Restaurant for coffee and just sat back and watched the show.

It would have taken me months, maybe years, to meet all the people I ran into there. I didn't know it at the time, but I would do business with many of them over the next few years.

There was probably never before as complete a gathering of criminals in one room in the United States as there was in the Green Lantern that night. There were escapees from every major U.S. penitentiary. I was dazzled. There were Tommy Holden and Francis Keating, two escapees from Leavenworth. They had taken a fall in a $90,000 mail train caper in Evergreen Park, Illinois. And Phil Courtney.

Gus Winkler was there. He was on the Syndicate's execution squad and he'd knocked off dozens of guys. He worked with Fred Burke, Johnny Moore, Shotgun George Zeigler, and Crane-neck Nugent, none of whom, to my surprise, were Italians. Everybody figured the Italians were the executioners. This was not so. Harvey Bailey was there too. He was suspected of being in the Denver Mint robbery and of robbing a bank in Lincoln, Nebraska. He was believed to have earned himself a cool two million on those capers.

For a kid like me, it was great stuff. Rogues Gallery, or

Hall of Fame. It depended on your point of view. But how could you *not* be impressed by Big Homer Wilson, who had been robbing banks for years and never had a fingerprint taken anywhere? Tommy Gannon was another phenomenally lucky robber who had never been made. Then there was Tom Philbin, the slot-machine kingpin, and Tommy Banks and Kid Can, out of Minneapolis, who ran alcohol and booze and had the gambling in Excelsior.

The later it got, the more the place jumped. There was so much goddamn noise at midnight that Sawyer had to yell out for quiet. He had the radio on and wanted to hear Ben Pollack's orchestra play "Auld Lang Syne."

Everybody got pretty sloshed, and at one point Frank Nash, a Leavenworth escapee, left to go to another party. At 8 A.M., he was back. Even when he was bombed, he always managed to look dignified. He'd always make sure, for instance, that his toupee was on straight. Anyway, he came running in with his overcoat pulled up around his neck and ran into Harvey Bailey, who was upset, to say the least.

"What bastard did this to me?" Bailey screamed, holding a shoe in his hand. He had taken off his shoes and gone to bed for a few hours and, while he was sleeping, somebody had nailed one of his big shoes to the floor. He'd had a hell of a job getting it loose.

"You think that's something?" Nash growled. He opened his coat and his tie was cut off an inch below the knot. "Which one of you bastards did that?"

Since Freddie and Doc and I spent so much time living in and around St. Paul and since we worked so closely with Sawyer and Peifer on various jobs, it was inevitable that we'd get dragged into the city's politics, even if it was on a minor level. We felt obliged to contribute something to keep the crooked guys in office because, as Peifer explained to us, we were partly responsible for strengthening the anticrime reform element in the city.

There was a growing reform movement reacting to the city's corruption, and they used the murder of Arthur Dunlop as a prime example that St. Paul was a crime capital. The Dunlop murder was a particularly messy job, and though Peifer and his men handled it, it was linked with Freddie and me and others who were getting to be notorious stickup men. Given the entire situation, it was only fair, as Peifer pointed out to us, that we contribute something to blocking the reformers.

Fortunately, Peifer only asked us for money, not muscle, and we gave gladly. But, at first, even the cash didn't help. In the election Peifer was concerned about, the election of 1932, a reformer named Mahoney was elected mayor, and he instantly demoted the chief of police and the chief of detectives. At that point Freddie and I decided St. Paul would not be healthy and made up our minds to leave the city and operate in another part of the Midwest for a few months. Peifer wasn't discouraged. He began planning for the following year's elections in Minneapolis. He and his cronies had a number of schemes, including the organization of a massive crime wave in the area that would discredit the reformers and their administration.

Freddie and I were busy with our own personal crime wave, and we didn't make another contribution to Peifer's plans until the Minneapolis election, when he again asked for money to back a candidate who was in the bag. We anteed up some cash, and this time Peifer and his contacts came through. Peifer's man won. Now the fix was to be in Minneapolis. It was possible to buy off anyone, as long as you came up with enough dough.

8

"No Woman of Mine Ever Got Around to Setting Up Permanent Housekeeping"

THERE WERE PLENTY of women in my life. I got married to one. I had a son by another. And I shacked up with a few others before, after, and in between.

I never showed my women a carefree, joyful time. When they hooked up with me, they just naturally bought trouble. I was forever installing them in an apartment, then rushing in suddenly in the middle of the night and ordering them to pack up. It was the familiar old story. We had to keep moving, and no woman of mine ever got around to setting up permanent housekeeping.

They also had their share of lonely times. I couldn't cart them everywhere. I'd provide them with a comfortable place to wait, and I'd send lots of cash when I had it, but I expected them to fill in their own hours until I came back. And sometimes I didn't ever come back. A thief has to select his girls from the world he moves in, and the broads you find there are likely to be making their own livings in some kind of underworld activity. I took up with a lot of whores in my time, but I never had any complaints about the personalities or morals or brains of any of them. And if my girlfriends weren't engaged in something criminal, then they were the daughters or sisters or cousins of burglars or holdup men or killers. I had plenty of them, too, and like the whores, you could trust them. Of course, I never introduced myself as a burglar or holdup man—I told my wife when we met that I was a jewelry salesman, which was, come to think of it, a pretty funny line—but inevitably they'd find out what my real business was, and I could always rely on them to play it smart with cops and other outsiders. We were all in the same general business and looked out for one another.

In many ways Herman Barker's widow, Carol Hamilton, set the style for all the women I was to know in my life. I met her for the first time in 1929 when I was just a kid, and she made an impression on me. She was beautiful. She was a full-blooded Indian, about thirty-five, with black eyes, even white teeth, and shiny black hair that dropped over her shoulders. She was five feet eight, and with her straight erect build, she stood out in any crowd.

Lawrence Devol introduced me to Carol, and he told me she was a really experienced woman. He was right. In her years with Herman, Carol had been through her share of run-ins with the cops. One time, she'd accompanied him on a job in Wyoming, and when he killed a policeman, Carol got a year in prison as an accessory. Carol understood my position when we first met—I was still on the lam from Hutchinson—and over the following few months, she used her contacts and experience to help me out in dozens of different ways.

First, she found me a place to live. She was staying in a

hotel named the Carleton in Sapulpa, Oklahoma. She was picking up a few dollars as a hustler, but she didn't say anything to me about that business. She just invited me into the Carleton to live. Later she moved into some rooms in West Tulsa, where the hustling was more lucrative, and she took me along. She introduced me to a couple of jobs, and when Devol got himself arrested in Ponca City, Carol put me in touch with the guy who somehow managed to spring him for only fifty bucks.

Carol knew her way around the shady side of the law, and she didn't mind sharing her knowledge with me. She also helped me in a more personal way. She took me to bed with her. I didn't have much experience in sex before I met her, but she taught me all her tricks, and I felt like a real man. She was a fantastic broad.

I didn't marry Carol, but she did the next best thing for me. She introduced me to the woman who eventually became my wife. Her name was Dorothy Slayman, and my introduction to her came in the spring of 1931. I'd just finished my term in Lansing, and I stopped in Tulsa on my way to look up Ma Barker to see Carol, who was living in a jazzy new apartment on North Cheyenne. She said she was running a massage parlor, which I took to be a fancy name for a hooker joint, and she had her niece staying with her. The niece was a redhead, about seventeen years old and beautifully stacked. Dorothy Slayman was one of the sexiest broads in Tulsa.

I fell for Dorothy the minute I laid eyes on her, and the attraction was mutual. Within a few days of our meeting, we'd been to bed together and we'd chosen our own personal love song. It was "You Were Meant for Me," and I believed every word of the lyrics. I played that record so often on Carol's crank-up phonograph that I wore the goddamn thing out.

I took Dorothy with me every chance I could, which, at

first, worked out to be most of the time. Much as I admired Carol, I was glad to move Dorothy out of the massage parlor atmosphere. I wasn't sure she was involved in the hustling business, but after we were together, I definitely didn't want her fooling around with other guys, even if it was on a business basis. My difficulty, of course, was that I couldn't offer her a life that was much of an improvement over her life with Carol. In some ways, it was rougher because I wasn't earning the kind of money that I needed to support her in style. Still, in our first weeks together, rough times or easy, nothing mattered to Dorothy, or to me, as long as we were together.

For most of 1931, when I wasn't away on a job with Freddie and the others, I was with Dorothy. Finally, in the fall, we got married. It wasn't any grand ceremony and we didn't take a special honeymoon, but after a couple of weeks I drove her up to Chicago to meet my family. We got a terrific reception. My father and mother and sister Emily turned out to welcome and congratulate us. My father even forgot to lecture me on my life of crime. Dorothy and I were so pleased we rented an apartment on the North Side and settled in.

It only lasted a couple of months. Dorothy enjoyed the quiet life in Chicago, but I began to feel the old familiar restlessness. I wanted to be on the move again. I wanted to swing back into action. I didn't tell Dorothy about my feelings. I lied to her. I said that winter was coming and that I'd have to join up with Freddie down South and organize a few scores before we ran out of money. Dorothy was hurt. She and Emily begged me to hurry back in time for Christmas. I said I'd try, but deep down I knew I'd never make it.

I didn't see Dorothy again for close to four years. I didn't mean to desert her in Chicago. I kept in touch by mail and I sent her cash from time to time. But circumstances and

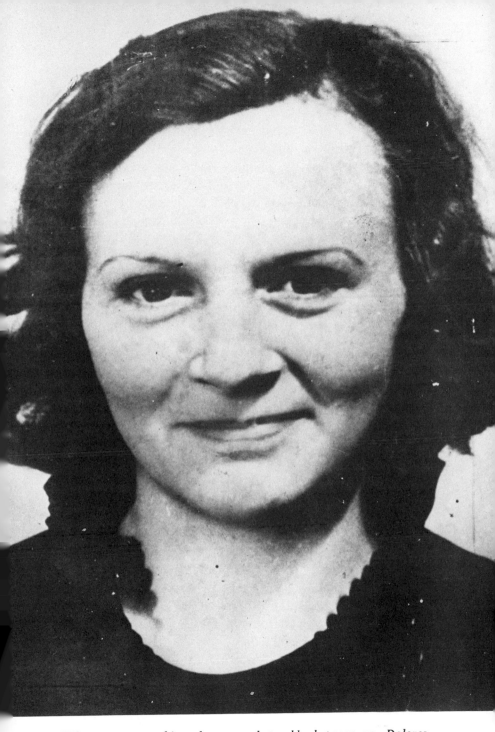

"There was something that caused trouble between us. Dolores refused to cook. I preferred home-cooked meals. I gave her a choice: 'Learn to cook or pack your bags.'" — UPI

the cops kept me away from her. And, on top of everything else, poor Dorothy stumbled into a bad break, something that neither of us could ever have anticipated. It, more than anything, kept us apart.

Who would have dreamed that she would step off the bus in West Plains, Missouri, on the very day that Freddie and Bill Weaver knocked off that sheriff? I'd written to her from the Barker farm near West Plains. I didn't invite her down, but she was so lonely that she hopped on a bus and arrived in West Plains only a few hours after the shooting. The state police were checking out every stranger, and naturally they picked her up. Somehow they connected her with me and threw her into jail. They didn't charge her with any crime. They just hoped that maybe I'd be fool enough to try to make contact with her. Then they'd nail me. I wasn't that stupid.

I heard about Dorothy's predicament when I was safely settled up in St. Paul. I felt sorry for her. But laying my neck on the line in a Missouri murder trial just didn't make sense. Besides, I knew that the cops wouldn't hold Dorothy for long. I also knew that wherever she went, the cops would keep a watch on her to see if I showed up. I couldn't risk seeing her again, at least not for a while, and mentally I said so long to my wife.

It wasn't many weeks after that I met another girl who hit me with a jolt. Her name was Dolores Delaney, and it was pure chance that I ran into her. I was still living in St. Paul, and Harry Sawyer asked me to deliver a parcel to a guy named Pat Riley, who often handled chores for Sawyer. I knocked on Riley's door, and this beautiful young girl answered. Riley was out, but the girl asked me in. We sat down and she played some records. She liked things like "Sweethearts on Parade." I could hardly speak. I just watched her. She was a brunette with brown eyes and a gorgeous figure. She was about sixteen.

Riley walked in.

"What's going on?" he said to me. "Are you trying to make my sister-in-law?"

"Why ask me a thing like that?" I said.

"Every guy wants to make her," Riley said, "but we've got a rule. Nobody gets into her pants until she's seventeen."

Well, at least I knew the rules. I came back and called on Dolores many times over the following weeks, but I never once so much as laid a hand on her. She was the youngest of three sisters. The older two were Babe Riley, Pat's wife, and Margaret, whose boyfriend was in the rackets. Dolores was the rebel of the family. She didn't like school, she didn't like her mother, and she was anxious to get out into the world. She was so undisciplined that her mother, whom I never met, finally stuck her away in a Catholic school for wayward girls.

The discipline didn't work. Dolores ran away from the school and made straight for Harry Sawyer's house. Sawyer sent for me. As soon as I walked in, Dolores jumped up and planted a big, juicy kiss on my lips. Dolores may have been a mere sixteen years as the calendar went, but as a woman, she was already plenty mature. I talked out the whole messy situation with Dolores and with Sawyer, and when I realized that there was no way Dolores would ever go back to her school or her mother, I asked her if she'd like to move in with me. She was ready to pack her bags the instant I spoke. But I held her off until we got an okay from Pat and Babe Riley. And from then on, until the police finally separated us three years later, Dolores and I were a steady couple.

Dolores was only a kid, but she amazed me by the way she handled herself in all the tough situations she had to face up to as the traveling companion of a holdup man.

Some things, though, I had to admit, got the best of her. She hated my traveling in the same way that Dorothy did. She also resented Ma Barker—somewhat the way some girls dislike their mothers-in-law. Ma felt the same way at first, but everybody got to like Dolores. After a couple of years, she even asked me to bring her over to visit her. But in the meantime, Dolores often bitched about the time I spent with Ma.

And there was something else that caused trouble between us. Dolores refused to cook. She insisted we eat every meal of the day in restaurants. I preferred home-cooked meals and ordered her to look after things in the kitchen. She argued and I often let her have her way. But as the police pressure mounted, as it grew more dangerous for me to walk around in the open, I told her that in towns like Chicago I had to avoid restaurants. I gave her a choice: "Learn to cook or pack your bags."

Dolores was stubborn. She packed her bags. I bought her a ticket for St. Paul and stuffed $1,000 in her purse. I took her to the train.

"You're really going to send me back home?" she asked.

"You're damn right," I said.

"Okay, I'll learn to cook."

We never talked about it again.

Dolores had as much nerve as she had good sense. When she was still only sixteen, she walked into a Minneapolis courtroom and gave Clarence Devol the alibi he needed to beat the beef of killing two cops. Lawrence Devol was already serving a life term for his part in those killings.

Dolores was seventeen when we found that she was pregnant, and again she showed her nerve. I arranged an abortion for her, and Dolores didn't shed a tear as she went off to have her operation.

She was probably bravest of all, though, when the heat

was really on me from the cops and the FBI in late 1934 and early 1935. We had to move fast and often in those months, and Dolores looked after her end without a whimper. She had plenty of reason to crack up, especially after she got pregnant again. She didn't complain, and she kept going. She decided that, on her second pregnancy, she wouldn't go for an abortion. But, under the conditions, with cops and feds all over the country looking for me, she couldn't settle down in any one place and wait out a normal nine-month pregnancy. She had to put in her nine months moving from place to place, and during that period we traveled through Ohio, Florida, Cuba, and half a dozen other places. We had no idea where the baby would actually be born.

I tried to make her pregnancy reasonably cheerful under the circumstances. I bought her a couple of dogs for company. One pup was a four-month-old toy bulldog, and Dolores took to him in a big way. We used to sit around in the evenings playing with the pup and listening to Lowell Thomas and *Amos and Andy* on the radio. It was a quiet, homey kind of existence, but we couldn't really relax like normal people. After all, we were only a couple of steps ahead of the police most of the time.

When the baby was finally born in February, 1935, Dolores was in police custody and I was still on the lam. The cops caught her in Atlantic City. I escaped. And when I read about the birth of my son, a seven-pound boy whom Dolores named Raymond Alvin, I was in a whorehouse in Toledo, shacked up with the madam.

Her name was Edith Barry, and she was the one who brought the papers in to me with the announcement about my kid's birth. Edith was another good broad. She knew I didn't love her—that all my thoughts were about Dolores. She just liked me and going to bed with me. It was a little tougher for me to get passionate with her. I'd been used to a firm young teen-ager, and Edith was about thirty years older than Dolores and not half as attractive. But I admired Edith. She knew her business, and she had the best connections in Toledo. The editor of the Toledo newspaper called in at her place regularly. So did all the elected politicians and the city's chief of detectives. Edith Barry's whorehouse, all in all, couldn't have been a safer place for a fugitive from the law like me. If trouble was coming, Edith would be the first to know and the first to warn me.

I knew I'd never see Dolores again, but I made one last effort to help her. I read in the papers that she was convicted on three counts of harboring a criminal, namely, Alvin Karpis, and she was handed three five-year sentences. She couldn't even keep her baby. The poor kid. For a few moments in hospital she held him in her arms and then he was given over to my parents. Dolores needed help, and at a fee of $10,000, I hired a lawyer in Dayton, Ohio, to appeal her sentences. The lawyer's name was Jack Egan and he had a reputation as a first-rate appeals attorney. But he had no success in Dolores' case. As soon as he began preparations, the FBI descended on him. They tapped his phone, shadowed him, harassed him. They didn't know for sure that I was paying him, but they suspected I was, and they wanted to scare him off the case. Eventually they succeeded. The appeal collapsed, and I realized that I would have to abandon Dolores the way I'd been forced to give up my wife, Dorothy.

I cleared out of Toledo after my negotiations with Egan collapsed and said good-bye to Edith Barry. But, not too amazingly, the next woman I took up with was another madam of a hooker joint. Her name was Grace Goldstein. She was a peroxide blonde of about thirty-five, and she ran the finest whorehouse in Hot Springs, Arkansas. Like Edith, she maintained great connections. The mayor of Hot Springs had a big crush on her. She entertained all the top crooks

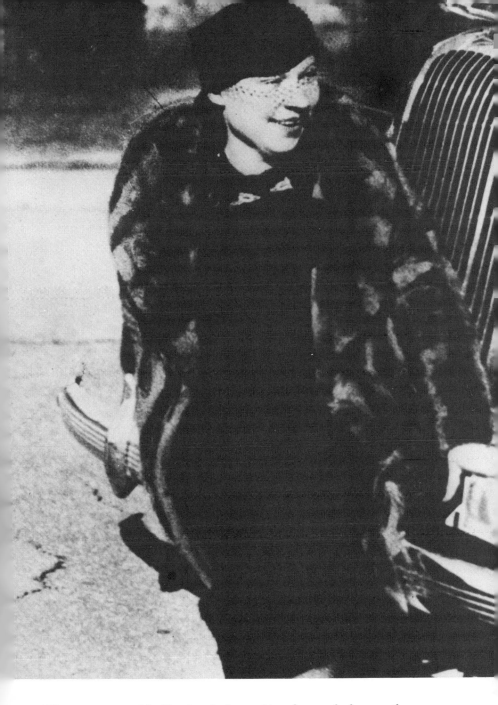

"She was a peroxide blonde of about thirty-five, and she ran the finest whorehouse in Hot Springs, Arkansas. Grace was a big leaguer." — UPI

who visited Hot Springs and all the top cops and politicians. Her establishment took up two floors of the Hatterie Hotel, which stood next door to the Arlington, the most luxurious hotel in town, and across the street from Mike Jacobs' Southern Grill, the town's most notorious gambling joint.

Grace was a genuine big-leaguer. She was also hot stuff in bed and helped me out in half a dozen other valuable ways. Whenever I wanted to visit Hot Springs, she rented a house for me, and it was always a comfortable, out-of-the-way cottage, where I had no worries. On top of her other attributes, she was tough. When the feds started breathing closer to me, they latched on to Grace. They put her through some rugged times and, for the most part, she stood up to them with a lot of courage.

Grace's experiences were typical of what all my women had to go through: I often felt guilty about the hardships I gave them and sometimes tried to spare them. In the summer of 1935 I went back to Dorothy to try to ease things at least a little for her. I found her in a town in Oklahoma and I told her to divorce me. She was bitter. I asked her what else I could do. She said she wanted to take a secretarial course that would cost $350. I gave her $500. I learned later that she took the course and that, on November 22, 1935, she got the divorce.

Poor Dorothy. Poor Dolores. Poor Grace. They all found out at one time or another that I was a crook and chose to stick by me. I loved each one of them.

"The hard times in the early 1930's made it tough to earn a dollar. One big drawback was the overcrowding in my business. Everybody wanted to be a crook." — WIDE WORLD PHOTOS

9
"The Depression Made Crime a Tough Proposition"

THE HARD TIMES in the early 1930's made it tough to earn a dollar in any line of work. The Depression even hit the criminals. But if you were a dedicated stickup man, if you worked hard, if you were determined to keep going in the face of all obstacles, and if you were smart in the choice of your partners and your associates, then you could eventually strike it rich. I was the living proof of the rewards that went with brains and perseverance. I hung in there and made it to the big money. Still, it wasn't easy, and the Depression, more than any other factor, made crime a tough proposition.

One big drawback was the overcrowding in my business. Everybody wanted to be a crook. The Depression threw farmers, salesmen, and factory employees out of work, and many of them tried crime to support themselves and their families. I read some statistics in 1936, published by the Justice Department, claiming that crooks outnumbered carpenters four to one, grocers six to one, and doctors twenty to one. I, for one, believed those figures. It seemed that every two-bit unemployed bum in the United States with the cash to dig himself up a pistol was taking a crack at the robbery business. The Midwest was the busiest area of all. All the states that bordered on the Mississippi River teemed with bandits trying to knock off the local banks and rural post offices. Crime was the last profession in America in the 1930's that still attracted crowds of applicants.

The difficulty for all of us real professionals was that ninety percent of the ex-farmers and unemployed salesmen and former factory workers who tried their hands at crime were amateurs. They needed money, but their hearts weren't really in the business of robbing and looting. So they failed at crime, and they made it tougher on the rest of us who were seriously involved in criminal careers. The bunglers only succeeded in making the cops, the bankers, the G-men, and honest citizens more alert to us professionals. With each year of the Depression, the banks grew harder to crack. The cops got smarter, the crime war got hotter, and I blamed the situation in large part on the amateurs crashing the field.

They were also a threat to your personal safety if you, as a professional crook, made the mistake of taking them along on a job. One day in 1931, when I was in Oklahoma, a fellow named Elmer Higgins asked me to his hotel room in the town of Jennings. I had the beginnings of a reputation then and Higgins had a proposition for me.

He was a big, easygoing fellow in his middle forties who'd worked in the oil fields. Higgins didn't look like a criminal, but he had gone with Sam Coker, a real professional, on a successful bank robbery up in Kansas. After his first taste of fast money, Higgins decided to forget the oil fields, where jobs were scarce anyway, and stick to robbing. He wanted to work with me, and he'd just begun to lay out his proposition, when the proprietor of the hotel came into the room to say that the town marshal was asking for him.

Higgins, his wife, and I trooped out to the lobby. The marshal was making a fuss about Higgins' car ownership, the car that had been used in the Kansas bank holdup, and he asked Higgins to walk down to the police station with him. Higgins agreed and said he'd just go back to the room and get his cap. Well, I knew that Higgins had a rifle and a pistol in his room, and I naturally figured that he'd bring them along, get the drop on the marshal, and we'd all clear out before the marshal found out too much about Kansas and the car.

Higgins came back with a cap on his head, and he and the marshal walked out to the street.

"You mean to say you're going to let the cop take my husband like that?" Mrs. Higgins said to me.

"What are you talking about?" I said. "Didn't he get his gun?"

"No."

The stupid bastard really had gone for his cap. I had to do something. I could see that Higgins would be arrested and I'd be marked down in Oklahoma as a guy who didn't back up his friends. I had no choice. I ran into the room, grabbed the rifle, and chased down the street. I caught the marshal from behind and jammed the rifle into his back. Higgins whirled around with his mouth yawning open. He was more stunned than the marshal. I disarmed the marshal right out there on the street and marched him back to the hotel room without anybody noticing.

The marshal was the Western type down to the last detail. He wore a big cowboy hat, a fancy holster, and a belt full of bullets, and he had a pair of brass knuckles in his pocket, covered with blood. He was tough, but I had the drop on

him, and with me directing Higgins, who was still bewildered, we managed to tie him up in the bedspread. Then
Higgins and I and his wife barreled out of town in his car.

We drove to a friend's house several miles from Jennings
and pulled up. I was still holding the rifle. It was a model
I wasn't familiar with, and I asked Higgins to show me how
to empty and load it. He took the thing and said that to
inject a shell you snapped this lever. He snapped the lever.
Nothing happened. I looked closer. There was no bullet in
the rifle. It was empty all the time I'd been pushing that
tough marshal around.

"My God, I forgot," Higgins' wife piped up. "I was afraid
the hotel lady's children would play with the gun, so I took
the bullets out."

I told Higgins right on the spot that there was no way
we could work together. He was an amateur, and he was
dangerous. I was right, of course, but I didn't realize at the
moment that he was a danger most of all to himself.

A few days later a friend told me Higgins was dead. He
and another guy had tried to hold up a drugstore in Oilton,
Oklahoma. The druggist pulled a gun. Higgins blasted away
with a shotgun and hit the druggist, his wife, and their baby.
The druggist caught Higgins with a twenty-five automatic.
Higgins died. So did the druggist.

The Depression didn't just affect the numbers and types
of people in the crime business. It also affected the size of the
profits you could earn. If the ordinary working guy wasn't
earning any money, then there was next to nothing for thieves
like me to rob. Oklahoma and Missouri were two states that
were really hard hit. Down there, everybody seemed to be
broke. In the early 1930's, the guys and I were forever busting
into store safes and coming away with next to nothing.

Sam Coker described the whole situation very accurately
one night in 1931. Sam was a first-rate burglar, and he and I

and Freddie went into Coffeyville, Kansas, for a few hours of thieving. We took a shoe store, a drugstore, a pool hall, and a gas station, and after all that effort, the loot, when we counted it, added up to a pitiful total of $150.

"This goddamn Depression is getting on my nerves," Sam said in his raspy voice. He had a queer way of talking. The story was that he'd been shot between the eyes during a poker game argument; the bullet dropped through to his throat and he spit it out. "I hate these bad times. I mean, we work like madmen, and all we have to show for it is chicken feed. It isn't just the workingman who's suffering. I'm sick of hearing that. Guys like us are having a hell of a time too."

Sam was right. It was hard enough to find a safe with any money in it, and when we stole merchandise, we often had trouble finding a buyer willing to pay a decent price. Jewelry, for instance, was just about impossible to unload. And so were a lot of other things in the luxury category.

In the case of that robbery back in Henryetta, Oklahoma, though, peddling jewelry happened to work to my advantage. The way things finally ended, I was glad we couldn't get rid of the watches and rings that Freddie and I had lifted. I would never have been able to make the deal with the original owner if I didn't still have the stolen merchandise, and if there'd been a normal, fast, good-paying underworld market in operation.

In the Depression years, law-abiding citizens didn't mind getting around the law where it meant money. The jeweler wouldn't have considered making a deal with me under ordinary circumstances. The jailer, who first brought up the matter of a deal with me, was a perfectly honest old fellow whose real business was farming, but he told me that he wasn't going to bother harvesting his crops because there was no place to sell them. He'd been forced to take a job as a jailer to get by and, what with no money and no crops market, he was willing to work out an arrangement for his friend the jeweler with someone like me—a guy he wouldn't have had anything to do with if times had been good.

Lots of otherwise honest people were on the criminals' side, or at least were sympathetic to them in those hard years. The bank-hating old North Dakota farmer who didn't object to our taking his car was another example of the attitude to crooks in the 1930's. We ran into that feeling all over. We never had trouble finding doctors to patch us up when we were winged in gunfights. They didn't care that they were looking after crooks, and we didn't have to worry that they'd rat on us to the police. After all, they knew that—unlike their other patients—we at least had the money to pay for their services.

Plenty of other citizens, it was true, reacted to the Depression in just the opposite way. They were the ones with a little money or property and, with people all around losing everything, they clung to what they had like bulldogs. They took strong and violent steps to protect their stakes against the crooks. These were the people who made up the fierce vigilante groups that sprung up all over the Midwest. Iowa was one of the worst states in the Union for vigilantes, and it was a wise crook who steered clear of those farm towns.

The vigilantes realized that the local sheriff or marshal couldn't protect their stores and the town bank all by himself and, to help him out, they organized themselves into police auxiliaries. All of them packed rifles and pistols in their stores and homes, and all of them had assigned duties. A couple of storekeepers always had the chore of acting as unofficial bank guards. In Fairbury, Nebraska, when we took the bank there, the guard was the druggist. We knew about him in advance, since it was always one of our key preparations to check out the armed guards before a job. We could be certain that once a guard spotted us from his store, he'd sound the alarm with a rifleshot, and all his fellow vigilantes would come running, armed to the teeth.

We didn't worry as much about the cops on some jobs as we did about those damn trigger-itchy vigilantes.

If I'd been an ordinary citizen during the Depression, I would have sided with the criminals. I would have been like many of the people in Oklahoma. I spent a lot of time there and I saw enough of the starving, miserable way they lived to realize that I would have been against any government that couldn't control an economic depression.

There was this family near Rush Springs, for example— three kids, a mother and father—and they lived on land as useless and depressing as a desert. It was hard and dry and parched from the sun, and sand blew across the roads in drifts like snow. Nothing grew out of the earth, and the few plants and vegetables that did make it to daylight looked as weak and lifeless as the people.

Their faces would have broken your heart. All the hope had gone out of them. They were the saddest faces I think I had ever seen. They were suffering. They were starving. When I sat down to dinner with them, I ate a little piece of salt pork and hot biscuits in some kind of white gravy. I stayed overnight, and next morning for breakfast I was served the same meal. Nobody could be healthy on that diet. And nobody could get anything out of the life on that land except grief and misery.

I took a gift up to the family, a brand-new crank-up vic-trola and fifty records, and it was the only time I saw any smiles. They were really happy. Something new and cheerful had come into their lives, and they shared it with all their neighbors. People poured in from all over the country to look at the victrola and listen to records. Word spread fast, and on the very night the victrola arrived, the family threw a big dance. They spread cornmeal across the rough wood floor. It was just as smooth as the floor of a ballroom after the cornmeal hit it, and the people danced all night long.

They whooped it up like it was New Year's Eve. It was a night of forgetting for them, and in the morning they went back to their rotten everyday routine.

It was enough to make me glad I was a criminal and not a starving Okie.

St. Paul Dispatch

Exclusive Service of the Associated Press

ST. PAUL, MINN., SATURDAY, JUNE 17, 1933.

HOME EDITION ☆ ☆ ☆

10 PAGES

PRICE TWO CENTS IN ST. PAUL

WORD FROM HAMM KIDNAPERS WAITED

Mrs. Sankey Denies Husband Has Part in Case

HOME OF KIDNAP VICTIM; TWO OF HIS SISTERS

SAFETY OF MILLIONAIRE ABDUCTION VICTIM TIES HANDS OF ST. PAUL POLICE

We've Withdrawn All Way From Case at Request of Family, but We'll Get Going Good After Seized Man Is Liberated, Dahill Asserts; Brewery Official Available Day or Night to Receive Message.

NEWS OF CRIME WITHHELD UNTIL AFTER PROMISED CONTACT WITH GANG FAILED

Mrs. Verne Sankey asserted today she does not believe her husband had anything to do with the kidnaping Thursday afternoon of William Hamm Jr., 39-year-old millionaire St. Paul brewer.

Meanwhile, the prisoner remained in the hands of kidnapers who demand payment of $100,000 ransom under threat of death.

Although another contact was reported established with the gang, associates of Mr. Hamm and his near

---

GUNMEN KILL 5 IN AMBUSH IN KANSAS CITY

Four Officers and Prisoner Shot Down by Machine Gunners.

FEDERAL AGENT WOUNDED

Ex-Chief Terrorized by Battle Before Union Station.

Kansas City, June 17.—Four officers and a prisoner were slain by machine gun fire and another officer was wounded in front of the Union station here today by gunmen who apparently sought to effect the liberty of Frank Nash, Oklahoma mail train robber being

10

"How Would You Boys Like to Work on a Kidnapping?"

JACK PEIFER LIKED throwing jobs our way, so Freddie and I weren't surprised when he asked us over to the Hollyhocks one afternoon in April, 1933, to talk over a score. The surprising thing was that Peifer, who usually came to the point right away, was leading into this one with a lot of palaver. Whatever it was he had in mind, I figured it must be a bombshell.

He went into a lot of elaborate explanation about the backgrounds of two guys named Shotgun George Zeigler and Monty Bolton. I already knew that Zeigler and Bolton were Chicago operators. They were, in fact, members of the Chicago Syndicate's execution squad, and both had been involved in the St. Valentine's Day Massacre of 1929. Al Capone's enemies from the near North Side were meeting in a garage on North Clark Street, and Zeigler, who had looked after many of the advance arrangements, planned to ambush them there.

It had been Zeigler's idea to use a car disguised as a police Cadillac touring car and to dress a couple of the killers in police uniforms, all of which was calculated to throw the victims off guard. Bolton was the lookout, and his job was to sit at the window of an apartment building across the street from the garage. As soon as the victims-to-be entered the garage, he was to signal Zeigler that it was time to take care of matters.

Well, the guys from the other gang arrived, and Bolton notified Zeigler. Bolton waited in the apartment until the executioners walked into the garage, then went out a back door, got into his car a block away, and took off. The execution went off on schedule, but the guy they wanted to knock off most—Bugs Moran, the leader of the near North Side outfit—miraculously didn't get to the garage in time.

Later, when I got to know Zeigler better, he filled me on the executions and the near-tragedy that occurred when they were disposing of the Cadillac after the caper. Zeigler assigned this last job to Anthony "Tough Tony" Capezio, a young hood who belonged to the Forty-two Gang on Chicago's West Side. Tony started dismantling the car in a private garage in an Italian neighborhood and, after removing all the upholstery, proceeded to cut up the body and parts of the engine with an acetylene torch. Well, Tony hadn't drained the vacuum tank attached to the outside part of the cowling under the hood and it exploded. Tony was blown clear to the ceiling of the garage, then came crashing down to the floor. He was stunned but not completely knocked out—and from then on they called him Tough Tony. The incident ended there, because in that neighborhood nobody dared call the cops for an explosion. In those days, it was an almost daily occurrence for an alcohol cooker to explode around there, since many of the area residents worked for the booze division of the Syndicate.

I met Tony a couple of years later and he told me that, as a reward, Al Capone had made him manager of the Silver Slipper, a notorious place out in Stickney, Illinois. Capone had that town under complete control. The Silver Slipper was a dime-a-dance joint, with fifty girls who'd gladly take you to a rooming house next door for a fee if you'd rather go to bed than dance. Poor kids—they'd do anything to keep from starving. I was in prison when I last heard about Tony. It was in the 1950's and he had been picked up by the police in San Francisco as a suspect in the killing of a Chicago hoodlum named Nick DeJohn, whose body was found stuffed in the trunk of a car. Tony had no trouble beating this beef even before it got off the ground.

Anyway, that day at the Hollyhocks, Jack Peifer went on to tell Freddie and me the strange story of Zeigler's younger days. He'd been an honor student and varsity football player at Northwestern University, until one day he threw everything away in one wild act. He apparently went crazy and raped a twelve-year-old girl in the basement of an apartment building. He couldn't explain why he'd acted in a way that had nothing to do with the kind of life he'd been leading. Zeigler was committed for trial, and while he was out on bail, he skipped. He disappeared completely. Then, several years later, he turned up as a member of the Chicago Syndicate. He was a hired killer and an associate of some of the top people in the organization, among them Frank "the Enforcer" Nitti, Phil D'Andrea, Lefty Louis, Jake Guzik, Denis Cooney, Murray "the Camel" Humphreys, and a guy they called "Little New York."

Because of the St. Valentine's Day incident, Zeigler had been Capone's fair-haired boy, but according to Peifer, both Zeigler and Bolton had fallen on tough financial times in 1932. Zeigler had lost a lot of money on the wheat market and he had been speculating with Bolton's money as well as his own. Now they were both short, and since they'd done a lot of favors for people around St. Paul in the past, Peifer suggested to Freddie and me that all of us in St. Paul should try to repay Zeigler and Bolton in some small way.

"All right, I suppose that's true," Freddie said, and I could see he was getting impatient, "but where do we come into it?"

Peifer leaned back with an extra-special important look and said, "How would you boys like to work on a kidnapping?"

Well, I didn't want to find myself tied into the rackets guys in any way. Neither did the rest of our guys. For one thing, they wouldn't let you steal. Stealing turned the heat on the Syndicate, and this they could do without. For another thing, I had no intention of becoming a hired assassin. Killing people for money didn't appeal to me or anybody connected with me. Apart from all that, the rackets guys were dangerous. I mean, if they got tired of you, well, Jesus, anything could happen.

But a kidnapping? I didn't mind the thought of that. I looked over at Freddie and I could tell he was thinking the way I was.

The three of us sat in Peifer's office for a couple more hours and talked out the proposition. There were plenty of risks. The kidnapping of Charles Lindbergh's baby son the year before had really put the heat on any kidnapping, because now the FBI had jurisdiction over this crime in cases where a victim had been transported across a state line. Crossing a state line was a technical violation of the law governing interstate commerce. Well, with this as a wedge, it was a sure bet the FBI would step in on this caper. All Hoover and his agents had to say was that they had confidential information that a kidnap victim had been taken from one

"Hamm [at left] was an okay guy. He sniffed the beer, tasted it again and held the stuff up to the light. 'I always say Hamm's is the best, but to tell you the truth, I don't know what the hell brand this beer is.'" — St. Paul Dispatch

state to another. The risks, we all realized, were probably higher than in any other job we'd ever pulled.

But the rewards made up for the dangers. Peifer figured we'd go for $100,000 ransom. He'd take a ten percent cut for coordinating the deal, and Zeigler, Bolton, Freddie, and I, and maybe a couple of other guys from the Karpis-Barker crowd would split the other $90,000. The thought of all that cash made sweet sounds in my head and in Freddie's, too, and before we left Peifer's office, he knew that he'd hired himself a couple of kidnappers.

Freddie and I almost forgot to ask Peifer one crucial detail. Who were we supposed to grab? The target, as it turned out, was to be a guy named William Hamm, Jr. Hamm was a bachelor, about thirty-eight years old, who lived in a big, old mansion on a hill in St. Paul. He was the president of the Hamm Brewing Company.

We knew Hamm was a rich man. Better than that, we knew, thanks to an act of the United States government, that he had a lot of hard, cold cash on hand. Not just stocks and bonds and jewelry and property—but good old every-where-negotiable U.S. currency. The government act that made his cash stock possible was the ruling in 1933 that breweries could sell beer with an alcohol content of 3.2 percent.

Well, Jesus, this was the beginning of the end of the dry era. Prohibition was now staggering on its last legs. Millions of thirsty Americans went wild in the rush to buy and drink the new powerful beer. All the breweries were doing a landslide business, and in St. Paul the Hamm plant was open twenty-four hours a day, trying to keep up with orders. And right now, the sales were all straight across the counter to individuals. Every sale was a cash sale, so needless to say, Hamm had quite a chunk of dough handy.

The deal looked solid to me, and I liked it even better after I met Zeigler and Bolton. They handled themselves like

"*We decided to conduct our operations from outside St. Paul, and Peifer rented a cottage at Bald Eagle Lake. We spent hours studying Hamm's habits. We got to know so much about the guy that I was sick of him long before the kidnapping.*"
— St. Paul Dispatch

what they were—big-time professionals. And I liked their looks, especially Zeigler's. He was a well-set-up six-footer, and he dressed in a snappier style than almost anyone I'd ever met. Zeigler gave you confidence, and he was smart enough to leave the matter of extra men on the job to Freddie and me, since we knew the St. Paul scene better than he did. We decided, in the end, that the job needed two more men, and we asked Doc Barker and Chuck Fitzgerald to join us. They accepted, and the six of us went to work.

We decided to conduct our operations from outside St. Paul, and Peifer rented a couple of cottages at Bald Eagle Lake. Early in May we settled into the place.

From there we made almost daily trips into St. Paul to case Hamm's brewery and home. We mastered every last detail of the layouts of both places and spent hours studying Hamm's habits, We got to know so much about the guy that I was sick of him long before the kidnapping.

Hamm's brewery stood in a gully, and the streets leading away from it ran uphill. His mansion sat at the top of one of the hills. Promptly at noon each working day, Hamm strolled out of his office, crossed a street, and headed up a sidewalk to his house. He took about an hour for lunch and returned along the same route. At night, close to six, he came out and took the identical walk home. After dinner, he went out on the town. He rarely stayed home, and his nighttime galivanting took him into any number of places.

It made most sense, in view of Hamm's night prowling that could take him anywhere, to snatch him off the street in the daylight just after he left his office. It was dangerous, but we laid such careful plans that, we figured, the actual grab would be quick and, to any possible passerby, harmless-looking. We would use an expensive car and dress me as the driver in a chauffeur's cap. Bolton, Fitzgerald, and Doc would accompany me. Doc and Bolton were merely insurance men standing across the street ready with their guns in case some disaster struck. Fitzgerald was to be the keyman at the outset.

Fitzgerald was an old hand who had taken part in a few Karpis-Barker scores. But what made him valuable for the Hamm deal was his looks. He was in his sixties, a real old-timer, and he had gray hair and a face that was nothing less than distinguished. His role was to stop Hamm in the street and invite him over to the car. We were certain that Hamm would think of Fitzgerald as some sort of businessman approaching him about an office matter.

Then with Hamm in the car, we'd beat it out into the country, where we'd meet a second car. Zeigler and Freddie would wait in it with some ransom notes for Hamm to sign, and as soon as he'd finished the paper work, we would cover his eyes with a blindfold and drive him to a hideout to wait for the delivery of the money.

The hideout called for another major decision. It couldn't be in any area near St. Paul, because Hamm might be able to reason out the location even with a blindfold on. We finally decided to use a house in Bensenville, Illinois. It was the local postmaster's house. While it meant bringing another guy into the plan, the postmaster, whose name was Batholmey, was completely trustworthy, and his house seemed ideal. Who would ever think of looking for a kidnap victim in a postmaster's home in Illinois?

The plan took shape through May and early June, and as a final precaution, Peifer put the fix in with a couple of his men at St. Paul's police headquarters. Freddie objected. He never liked bringing a cop into one of our capers. But Peifer explained that if the police tried to lay a trap when we went to pick up the ransom money, his contacts would let him know instantly and he'd get word to us.

It made sense. The ransom notes specified that the money was to be dropped out of a Hamm Brewing Company truck on a certain empty stretch of highway, but there was no way we could guard against a police ambush if they took it into their heads to blast us. We could have knocked off Hamm in retaliation, but what we wanted was the money, not a dead millionaire. Peifer's crooked cops at headquarters were insurance against any police funny business.

The day of the grab was set for June 15, and it came off right on schedule. What a performance Fitzgerald put on that day. It was a masterpiece! We parked the limousine in the street outside the brewery just before noon, and while Doc, Bolton, and I took up different positions near the car, Fitzgerald crossed the street and approached Hamm as he stepped out of the front door of the brewery.

"Mr. Hamm," Fitzgerald said, sticking out his hand, "I wonder if I might speak to you on a rather important business matter."

Hamm was shaking hands and nodding without really knowing what he was doing. He fell for Fitzgerald hook, line, and sinker. And Fitzgerald, never letting go of Hamm's hand, eased him the few feet over to our car and slid him into the back seat so smoothly that Hamm didn't raise a question. The rest of us slipped into our seats at the same time, me behind the wheel, Doc beside me, Bolton and Fitzgerald on either side of Hamm, and we pulled away.

"I don't like to do this, Mr. Hamm," Fitzgerald said, "but I'm going to have to ask you to get down on the floor because I don't want you to see where you're going. I hope you don't mind."

I looked at Hamm in the rearview mirror. He didn't look like a man who suspected he was a kidnap victim. He seemed to think that someone was making a mistake. Hamm was genuinely puzzled, but he did what Fitzgerald told him. He kneeled down on the floor of the car.

"Please don't try to look out, Mr. Hamm," Fitzgerald said in his cool controlled tone. "I'll tell you when you can sit up."

"*I weighed the chances of an ordinary passerby just happening to recognize Doc or me, just happening to wonder why the hell one of the passengers in the car had dark glasses and balls of cotton over his eyes. I felt tightened up for the whole drive.*"
— St. Paul Dispatch

We reached the second car in twenty minutes. Zeigler and Freddie were waiting with the ransom notes. There were four of them, all identical, typed by Zeigler, and we showed them to Hamm. The notes authorized payment of $100,000, and they asked that it be made quickly and guaranteed Hamm's release, unharmed, immediately on delivery of the cash in the manner specified in the notes. Hamm read one note, checked the others and, without asking any questions, signed all four.

Doc took some cotton balls out of the glove compartment of the first car. He told Hamm to shut his eyes and he pressed the cotton against Hamm's eyelids. He covered the cotton with a pair of dark glasses, and Hamm didn't see a road, a house, a tree, or a trace of sunlight all the way to Bensenville.

We took all kinds of precautions at Postmaster Bartholmey's place. We'd instructed him to send his wife and daughter away for a visit, and he himself slept on the sofa in the downstairs living room. He was allowed upstairs only to use the bathroom, and in the five days we stayed in Bensenville, Bartholmey and Hamm never once laid eyes on each other. We boarded up the window in the bedroom where we kept Hamm, and during his waking hours we made him sit at a table that faced the wall and away from the door. We didn't want to give him the chance to take too many long looks at any of us.

I stayed with Hamm for the entire period we held him. The others were in and out, except for Freddie and Zeigler, the two guys who looked after the collection of the ransom. I didn't mind my job. Hamm was no trouble. In fact, he was a model prisoner, and I did my best to make him feel reasonably at home. The bedroom was hot with the window boarded up, and I brought him a fan. I brought him books and back copies of the *Saturday Evening Post*. And from time to time, I brought him a bottle of beer.

I was worried about that beer. There wasn't any Hamm's beer in the house, and I didn't want to offend him by serving a rival brand. I finally poured him another company's beer, but I washed the labels off the bottles. He drank the beer without making a comment. Finally, after a couple of days, I got a little curious.

"Can you tell by the taste if it's your beer?" I asked.

"That's a good question," he said, and he laughed. He sniffed the beer from the bottle, tasted it again, and held the stuff up to the light. "I always say that Hamm's is the best but, to tell you the truth, I don't know what the hell brand this beer is."

Hamm was an okay guy. He was concerned about his release because, he said, it was a busy time of the year around his office. But I could tell he wouldn't even consider trying anything tough with me. The only worry I had didn't come from Hamm but from a newspaper headline. It was a hot item about Frank Nash, a stickup man who'd accompanied Freddie and me on a number of bank jobs. According to the story, FBI agents had arrested Nash in Hot Springs. They took him back to Kansas City to face a long list of charges and just as they were walking out of Union Station in Kansas City, a guy packing a machine gun jumped in front of them. The gunman, working alone, had plenty of nerve. His job was obviously to rescue Nash, and he turned his gun on the FBI agents and mowed them down. But his aim was lousy. He hit a few innocent bystanders too. And, instead of rescuing Nash, this gunman killed him and then disappeared.

The story hit me hard. First, I was sorry that Nash was killed. Second, I knew that the cops would be out in force. The FBI had been disgraced. One of their agents was dead and another wounded. And the feds didn't take that kind of embarrassment lightly. They would be raiding every joint and shaking down every known burglar in the Midwest. Their campaign wouldn't make it any easier on a gang of kidnappers. The FBI might conceivably pick one of us up and, even worse, their general dragnet could make it tougher to release Hamm, especially for the driver assigned to look after the release. The driver happened to be me.

Freddie and Zeigler, meanwhile, were having their own problems. From Bensenville they had gone back to the St. Paul area to wait for the appointed time to meet the brewery truck on a specified stretch of highway. The truck was to drop the money for Zeigler and Freddie. But Peifer phoned them with a warning a few hours before.

"Don't meet the truck," Peifer said. Peifer had heard from one of his police contact men that the cops were laying a

"I was in the postmaster's house keeping an eye on Hamm. Freddie and Zeigler came up the walk with a heavy briefcase and great big smiles. 'You round up some of Hamm's beer,' Zeigler said. 'I got a feeling it'll be my favorite brand for a long time.'"
— ST. PAUL DISPATCH

trap. They were going to station a machine gunner under the truck's tarpaulin. Zeigler and Freddie stayed home. They worked out details of a new dropping spot for the money and instructed the delivery man to drive a car that they described carefully. It had to be a Chevrolet coupe, and it had to be stripped of all the side doors and the door on the trunk. If the cops planned to send along another machine gunner, this guy would have to sit out in plain view.

The stripped-down car was Zeigler's idea, and it was a brilliant stroke. The pickup went off without a hitch. No machine gunners. No tailing cops. No planes overhead. No trouble. A clean getaway.

I was in the postmaster's house, keeping an eye on Hamm, when I heard Zeigler's car pull into the driveway. I hustled downstairs and opened the door. Freddie and Zeigler were coming up the walk with a heavy briefcase and great big smiles.

"You better round up some Hamm's beer," Zeigler said. "I got a feeling that it'll be my favorite brand for a long time to come."

My God, we were happy that day. We whooped and hollered as we opened up the briefcase and spread out the money. There was no doubt that we had $100,000, all in crisp U.S. bills. Bartholmey, the postmaster, walked in, saw the money, took another look, and toppled over on the sofa in a kind of daze.

I finally threw a damper on the celebration. Since it was my job to engineer the release, I was anxious to settle the plan of action. Freddie said that the hunt for the gunman who knocked off Frank Nash and the FBI agents was concentrated in the Kansas City area, but that things were tightening up around St. Paul. The cops and the feds were getting jumpy. I didn't like the sound of that, and I decided on a slight rewrite of our original plan for dumping Hamm.

In the first place, I asked to have Doc and Bolton ride

along in the car with Hamm and me for protection. In the second place, I changed the location for dropping him off. The original idea was to take him back to St. Paul. But there was no way anything could lure me into that town. I said I'd drive him out into the sticks, way in the back-country, and I didn't get a word of disagreement from anyone.

I let Hamm know he was going home. I told him to have a bath and, while he was in the tub, I took four twenty-dollar bills out of his wallet and substituted four twenties from the ransom money. If the bills were hot, if the cops had recorded the serial numbers, then Hamm would be the first to pass them. The St. Paul papers would report the news that the bills had turned up in the city, and we'd know right away that we'd have to be cagey about the rest of the cash.

We left Bensenville at six in the evening, Hamm, Doc, Bolton, and I, and we drove all night. It was a nerve-wracking trip. I worried about highway patrols. I thought about the chances of the feds scouring in the areas we passed through. I weighed the chances of an ordinary passerby just happening to spot us driving along the highway, just happening to recognize Doc or Bolton or me, just happening to wonder why the hell one of the passengers in the car had dark glasses and balls of cotton over his eyes. I felt tightened up inside for the whole drive, and I knew all the time that Hamm could sense my anxiety.

I drove from Bensenville up into Wisconsin, through Madison, into a little town called Taylor Falls, out the other side, and over to a small place in the state of Minnesota by the name of Wyoming. It was eight in the morning, and I'd driven far enough. I told Hamm that I was letting him out, and I spoke to him as a man I'd come to like and respect, even if our relationship was a strange one, kidnapper to victim.

"I'd like you to wait here ten or twenty minutes before you

make a phone call," I told him. "I'd appreciate it if you'd give us that much time."

Hamm was still wearing his eye cover. He was sitting in the car, facing straight ahead, very still, and he took a long time to answer.

"I don't think I could ever identify any of you fellows," he said.

I let him out of the car, slammed the accelerator, and headed toward Illinois. I hit Elmhurst, Illinois, and let Bolton out. He lived in the town and he pointed out a house down the street that was done up in the front yard like a beautiful, manicured city park garden. It was Shotgun George Zeigler's

"He took a long time to answer. 'I don't think I could ever identify any of you fellows,' he said."
William Hamm (RIGHT) *shortly after his release*
— ST. PAUL DISPATCH

home. He was a landscape gardener in his spare time. Would wonders never cease? But I was too tired to marvel at Zeigler's talents. I kept on driving until Doc and I reached Chicago.

All of us conspirators met a day later in Fitzgerald's apartment on the North Side of Chicago. The money added up to $100,000. But was it hot? We argued the pros and cons of splitting it up right then and there and letting each guy spend his share as he felt like it. Or should we wait until Hamm passed the twenties that I'd planted in his wallet?

We finally settled on a middle plan of action. We assumed the police really had marked the money. Our best choice, we figured, was to peddle the money to a dealer who specialized in hot currency for the usual five percent handling fee. Peifer spoke up and said he'd be willing to cut his share of the take from ten percent to five. The rest of us poured him another drink in thanks, and a few days later I flew out to Reno and sold the money to a couple of dealers I knew. Reno money was safer money, even if it was $5,000 less than Hamm money, and back in Chicago we got together and split it up in equal shares.

We had our cash, but all of us put in a few worrying days while we looked around for good times to spend it on. It seemed that every time I picked up a paper or talked to a friend in the early summer of 1933, I read or heard something that brought my mind back to the Hamm job. I couldn't get away from it.

First there was the kidnapping of John Factor. He was a rich character they called Jake the Barber, and he was another Midwest snatch victim. The ransom date was set for some time around July 12, and the cops deposited the money, $70,000, according to the kidnappers' instructions. But they also surrounded the area with a plane, cars, and close to fifteen hundred cops. It didn't do them any good. The crooks grabbed the cash, shot it out with the army of policemen, and made a clean getaway. The cops were disgraced again.

I admired the guts the Factor kidnappers showed. But at the same time, I knew the cops would be infuriated by the escape and turn the heat on every known crook in the business.

The heat was certainly up to boiling temperature in the Chicago area. The hunt for the killer of Frank Nash and the FBI agents had moved north from Kansas City to Chicago suburbs like Cicero, Maywood, and Melrose Park, where crooks traditionally hung out. According to rumors, the police had definitely pinned down the identity of the killer. He was none other than Vern Miller, the guy who did the spectacular driving job after the stickup of the Northwestern Bank in Minneapolis. Miller was the man the cops wanted and, to help root him out, they tapped and bugged so many telephones around Chicago that it wasn't safe to say more than hello and good-bye into any receiver in the entire city. I decided to lie low and keep my mouth shut. Vern Miller had too many associations with the Karpis-Barker crowd for me to show my face where the cops were.

All of the Hamm kidnappers played it cool, but no amount of precaution could have saved Monty Bolton from the weird, once-in-a-million situation he ran into. He was flying some hot bonds from Chicago over to St. Paul to see if Peifer could peddle them and, as he was looking for a seat on his plane, he spotted a familiar face coming on board. It was William Hamm, Jr. Bolton didn't know whether Hamm would recognize him, but for the entire trip, he sat there in panic. He was so nervous that he walked back to the washroom and hid the bonds. And he didn't wait out the flight to St. Paul. When the plane touched down in Madison, Bolton retrieved his bonds and hopped into the airport. Hamm flew on to St. Paul alone.

Finally, in late July, the pressure eased. The cops nailed the notorious Touhy Gang, and that victory raised their stock. It was only a stroke of bad luck that landed the gang in the hands of the police. Roger Touhy and three others were driving along a highway near Elkhorn, Wisconsin, when they skidded off the road and slammed into a telephone pole, A policeman came along and ordered them to follow him to the police station. This they did. A search of their car revealed handcuffs and adhesive tape, tools of the kidnappers' trade, and some weapons.

A few days went by, and then J. Edgar Hoover himself announced from Washington that his men had put together a solid case against Touhy's boys. The scientific evidence left no doubt at all, Hoover said, that the Touhys were the men behind the kidnapping of William Hamm.

I had to laugh—because the feds were so wrong, and because the heat was off. It was the end of weeks of pressure, and the situation looked even brighter when a grand jury in St. Paul followed through on Hoover's announcement by indicting Touhy and his guys for the kidnapping. Touhy may have been responsible for a lot of crimes, but one job he was definitely *not* responsible for was the grabbing of William Hamm.

When the Touhy trial came to court in November, the jury brought in a verdict of not guilty for the whole gang. Hoover wasn't too happy about the result. I didn't care. I'd moved on to other jobs, other crimes. The Hamm kidnapping was just ancient history to me. Just one more successful Karpis-Barker production.

St. Paul Pioneer Press

Exclusive Service of the Associated Press.

ST. PAUL, MINN., WEDNESDAY, AUGUST 30, 1933.

HOME EDITION ☆ ☆

18 PAGES

PRICE TWO CENTS IN ST. PAUL

COP SLAIN, ANOTHER SHOT IN $30,000 SOUTH ST. PAUL MACHINE GUN RAID

In Contract, says expert. Read Ely Culbertson's article on this topic on Page 10 today.

south, becoming northwest, and south.

VICTIMS AND SCENE OF PAYROLL ROBBERY

1 OF 5 BANDITS BELIEVED WOUNDED BY POLICEMAN AS BATTLE RAGES IN STREE

Gang, Confronting Bank Messengers as They Emerge From Postoffice With Payroll, Disarm, Then K Escorting Officer; Firing Begins When Second Patro man Starts in Car to Take Up Post as Guard but Struck Down at Wheel.

LONE MACHINE GUNNER RAKES STREET, SENDING BYSTANDERS SCURRYING TO COVE

Behind a barrage of machine gun, shotgun and pis bullets which killed one policeman and wounded anoth seriously, a bandit gang of five members snatched $30,000 payroll from two bank messengers at 9:45 A. today in South St. Paul. A bandit is believed to have be wounded in the firing.

The slain patrolman, Leo Pavlak, 38 years old, killed by shotgun slugs after one of the bandits had tak his pistol. The other officer, John Yeaman, was stru in the face by machine gun bullets and was sy

11

"Chicago Blues"

FOR A PLAIN Kansas boy like me, Chicago in the last months of 1933 was sometimes a hell of a place to operate. Partly it got me down, I suppose, because it was the city. I liked the wide-open spaces of Oklahoma and Kansas. I was used to making a getaway from bank jobs through fields and farmers' yards, over dirt roads, and across dry creek beds. In the city, in Chicago, it was all asphalt and traffic and big buildings. And it made a difference to me.

Part of the trouble in the North that fall of '33 for me was simply the speed of events. A lot of things semed to happen in a short space of time. Guys I knew were shot, wounded, knocked off by Chicago Syndicate operators. There were mob killings, jobs that fizzled out, pressure from a lot of different directions.

Our gang started off the autumn by traveling to St. Paul and sticking up the South St. Paul Post Office. The operation involved robbing three employees as they carried money down a street between the post office and a bank, which seemed easy enough. But it was complicated by the fact that three cops in two cars always acted as guards. Those cops made Freddie jumpy before the job got under way and, sure enough, at the zero hour, shortly after nine o'clock one morning, Freddie came out shooting.

He was using a machine gun and he sprayed everything in sight. He hit one of the two cop cars while it was moving, and it careened out of control, jumped a curb, ricocheted off a building, and bounced to rest in the middle of the street. Freddie blasted bits out of the buildings, peppered a streetcar that lurched onto the scene, and he even nailed a couple of cops.

The cops and bank guards shot back. They fired from the street and from windows in the post office, and the goddamn area seemed to be raining bullets. I don't know why half the gang wasn't knocked off. Poor old Chuck Fitzgerald was the only guy who caught a shot. It hit him in the hip, and he could barely drag himself into the car for the getaway.

Fitzgerald took a shot of morphine and a long gulp of booze to ease the pain, and in Calumet, Illinois, on the route from St. Paul to Chicago, he finally got to see a doctor who said that his age made the wound serious.

Fitzgerald was bound to be laid up for a long time, but we had a kind of informal health insurance scheme. As long as Fitzgerald was out of action, he'd keep on receiving a share of the jobs we pulled off. In the meantime, he'd earned a fair-sized chunk from the South St. Paul Post Office score. The total take added up to $3,000 in coins and $30,000 in paper money, a good day's work, even if it did cost one wounded crook and, as we found out from the papers, one wounded and one dead cop.

Fitzgerald wasn't the only friend who took a bullet during those months. There was a guy I knew around Cicero, Illinois, named Gus Winkler. He was a Chicago operator, a great bank robber, a member of the Chicago Syndicate's execution squad, and a man I had a lot of respect for. But somebody in Chicago didn't care for him, and Gus was cut down by a couple of blasts from a shotgun while he was standing outside a wholesale beer joint that he owned.

Gus had got caught up in a crazy situation. After that famous $2,000,000 Liberty Bond robbery in Lincoln, Nebraska, Gus and three other guys were arrested and charged with the robbery. Well, these four guys were innocent and Al Capone was in a rage that one of his best men might go to prison on a bum rap. Capone passed the word around that those responsible for the Lincoln robbery had better come up with those bonds. Big Al wanted to make a deal with the Burns Detective Agency people whereby, in return for the recovery of the Lincoln bonds, Gus would be released and the charge against him dropped, In the end, Capone agreed to pay $35,000 to the real bank robbers for the paper. The bonds were turned over to Capone and Gus was released as soon as the bonds had been restored to the rightful owners, the bank. As it turned out, though, the bank never recovered from the robbery and finally had to close its doors. The three other guys arrested with Gus were convicted and served many years in the Nebraska State Penitentiary on a bum rap.

After this affair, Capone seemed to have a soft spot in his heart for the professional bank robbers from that part of the country, and all during his heyday they were welcome in Cicero. After the feds nailed Al for income tax evasion, though, things changed and the Syndicate took a hard stand with us common thieves. A good example of the way they felt occurred after the shoot-out in Little Bohemia. Dillinger, Nelson, Hamilton, Homer Van Meter, and Tommy Carroll escaped an FBI trap and Hamilton was shot in the back.

"Capone seemed to have a soft spot in his heart for the professional bank robbers, and all during his heyday they were welcome in Cicero." — UPI

The Chicago Syndicate gave strict orders that no one was to give aid to this group, but the owner of a beer joint let them hole up in a back room for a few days until they could arrange to go to Volney Davis' apartment in Aurora, Illinois. The final outcome was that Hamilton and Dillinger stayed in Volney's apartment until Hamilton died from gangrene and was taken out and buried by Dillinger and some of our guys. Dillinger, a quiet guy with a gentle manner and speech, sat reading Street and Smith Western stories while Hamilton waited for death. There was nothing Dillinger could do. No doctor was going to treat Hamilton and run the risk of bringing the Syndicate's wrath down on him.

One time I almost got cut down myself in Chicago. Some Syndicate hoods called me in for a meeting in the offices of the Motion Picture Operators Union, a hangout of theirs, and told me they were out to knock off some of the guys in the Touhy Gang. They thought I was a Touhy member. I wasn't. It just happened that I knew a couple of Touhy people out in the Long Beach area and I had tipped them off to be careful what they did since the Syndicate didn't like having robbers around.

Frank "the Enforcer" Nitti, Phil D'Andrea, and Willie White, three of the big boys of the Syndicate, wanted to know why I'd tipped the Touhy guys off. I said I didn't want my friends killed. They were burglars, not rackets guys.

"We're going to give you a pass," DeAndrea said finally, and this relieved me, because the way those guys were slouched over those easy chairs staring at me, I was a little on edge, to say the least.

"There was one guy among you," Nitti cut in. "One guy among you was in the rackets."

"Can you guess?" Willie White asked. The other guys grinned.

The room was kind of dark and I couldn't quite see White's

face as he sat at the desk, and now I was wishing I were somewhere else.

"Vern Miller," White said.

"I didn't know you were hot at him," I said.

Nitti, who had been sitting on the arm of a chair, got up, walked over to the desk, and sat down on the corner of it. "Everybody's hot at that bastard," he said. I looked around, but now nobody was laughing or grinning.

That was the end of the meeting and I was glad to get out of it. But soon after, Vern Miller went the way of Gus Winkler. I hadn't seen Miller since shortly after his episode with Frank Nash in the Kansas City railroad station. I hadn't any idea where he was hiding out until the report came through that his body had turned up in a ditch near Detroit. Some guys had hit him on the head, stabbed him, wrapped his body in a blanket, and dumped it in the ditch. The details made it seem to me like a Chicago job even though it was carried out in Detroit.

Things never seemed to go right in Chicago, but there was nothing to equal the disaster of the Federal Reserve Bank caper late in 1933. It had been Shotgun George Zeigler's idea. He had been playing the wheat market again and was short of money.

Every night between eleven thirty and midnight, a messenger rolled a pushcart out of the main post office in downtown Chicago. Two guards then accompanied him to the Federal Reserve Bank, which was the next building along the street.

"What makes you so sure there's money in that cart?" I asked Zeigler.

"The guards," he said. "Why else would they be there?"

Well, that made sense. Anyway, one night I scouted the area. I drove into the loop on Jackson Boulevard and had a look at the Federal Reserve Bank, then went on to Clark and Adams to see the post office. It was a huge building that took a whole block, and on the Jackson Boulevard side there was a tunnel for registered mail trucks. The trucks were armored and had bulletproof glass.

Why would they use a pushcart when they had all those armored trucks? I couldn't figure it out. But, just before midnight, sure enough, the guy came out of the post office with the cart. He was accompanied by two plainclothesmen. They walked to the bank and were let in immediately.

This job appealed to me, and I took the matter up with Freddie and Doc. They liked the idea too, and the next time I saw Zeigler I told him we were in. Zeigler let me do most of the talking. If it had been a kidnapping, he would have been capable of planning it. But not a heist. That was *our* kind of business.

My main concern was to settle on a place to run after the stickup. Zeigler solved the problem. He knew of a little property north of Elmhurst, outside Chicago, which we could buy for practically nothing. There was a dance hall and bar and at the rear a garage with living quarters above it.

While we negotiated for the place, Zeigler and I ran the roads. There was one obvious problem that could cause us trouble: heavy traffic on Jackson Boulevard, even at midnight. But I came up with an answer to that one. I suggested planting a second car on the boulevard. It would be rigged with a device that would blow smoke all over the street. With this smoke screen blocking traffic, we could easily slip away.

I really put some effort into this caper. We had a portable typewriter now and put the details of our route down in a businesslike way. The route markings made me a little nostalgic for the open country of Kansas, Missouri, and Oklahoma. Our maps once showed trees and rivers and farmhouses as markers. Now our guideposts were street corners and big slabs of real estate.

The car was another part of the preparations and this

called for a lot of finesse. It was a Hudson—but not just an ordinary Hudson. Our favorite Chicago underworld garage had equipped it with a few accessories. The mechanics added bulletproofing, a shortwave radio, and a button in the glove compartment that slid open a panel in the driver's door. This was a handy opening for gunplay.

We added one more wrinkle to the Hudson. We equipped it to look like a car from the state attorney's office. The attorney's men often raided places in search of known hoodlums, and in this they worked with an organization known as the Secret Six, a crime-busting outfit headed by Pat Roche. They drove vehicles that were instantly identifiable by their headlights, one red and one green, and by the red star on the spotlight. We had our car decorated in the same way. Anybody seeing us in a car like that would automatically assume we were agents off on a raid.

The night before the caper, Freddie, Monty Bolton, Weaver, Doc, Harry Campbell, and I gathered at Zeigler's place in Berwyn, just west of Cicero. It was decided five guys would go on the job, thus assuring sufficient firepower. But who would the five be? That took a little discussion.

We ruled Campbell out right away. He had just arrived from Oklahoma and wasn't familiar with the details. That left six men. Well, Zeigler insisted that his friend Bolton had to go, and Freddie said Doc had to go, and eventually I was the one who dropped out.

The next night the guys went into action. As soon as the messenger came out of the post office with the plainclothesmen, Freddie and Zeigler went for them. They took the guns from the cops, grabbed the mailbags, and threw them into the Hudson. At the same time, Doc pulled the smoke car, a Dodge, out into the center of Jackson Boulevard, and instantly it belched a thick cloud of black, greasy smoke. It looked like an Oklahoma oil well on fire.

The guys congratulated themselves on a perfectly executed

heist, as they piled into the Hudson and followed their route plan: one block west, one block north, through an alley, left turn on Adams, through the loop, across the river and Canal Street, straight west on Adams.

＼ Then when everything seemed under control, this goddamn car, traveling in the opposite direction, tried to squeeze past, and the Hudson rammed into it and there was a hell of a crash. The area was the local skid row and the cops usually walked three abreast. They were on the scene before the guys could get out of the car and the shooting started.

Doc let fly with a 380 automatic through a side window. Bolton cut loose with a machine gun, and the first guy he hit was Doc. He caught him in the hand and Doc let out a yell.

During the shooting, Freddie and Weaver commandeered a Buick that happened to be passing by, and everybody piled guns, ammunition, and mailbags into it and took off.

As they swerved onto Ashland Avenue, Doc noticed that the Buick's gauge indicated a quarter tank of gas. Another car would have to be grabbed, and hopefully it would have more gas. At Forty-eighth and Ashland, they shocked a man and woman out of their wits by unceremoniously bouncing them out of their new Ford four-door sedan into the street. Again the equipment and the mailbags were transferred. This time they were lucky. The gas gauge registered nearly full. The stunned couple just stood there gawking as their car sped off.

The guys finally made it to the hideout in Elmhurst and there they began adding up the losses. They had abandoned the Hudson and, with all the money poured into it for gimmicks and accessories, it was a big loss. Then, too, somewhere along the way, probably during one of the frantic car switches, they had left behind a fifty-shot drum for one of the machine guns and a large sample case of forty-five automatic shells.

They weren't happy about their losses, but they figured they would be small compared with the loot. Then they started opening the mailbags and, Jesus, the first one had nothing but checks, and so did the second and third. Frantically, they ripped into all the bags and every one of them contained nothing but checks. Checks were useless to robbers. They couldn't be cashed.

The whole goddamn haul hadn't brought in a nickel of hard cold cash. Worse than that, it had cost the outfit a hell of a sum. Everybody agreed the caper had been a total fiasco.

The next morning the newspapers told the grim story. The headline in the Chicago *Tribune* put it all down in six words: TEN THOUSAND POLICE HUNT COP KILLERS.

Apparently Bolton had killed one of the cops when he opened up with his machine gun. He had done all the damage on that job. Doc was sore at him for the shot that caught him in the hand. Not that he minded the wound so much, because the bullet had only skinned him. But the shot had blown a big diamond right out of his favorite ring, and for this he was plenty mad.

The main worry was over the car. No one could identify the guys, so the cops couldn't possibly link them directly with the heist. But they might have left something behind in the car. Fingerprints maybe.

Luckily, the guys got a break. Skid row bums had descended on the car after the bandits abandoned it, and before police reinforcements arrived they had picked it clean. They didn't leave anything they could carry away and, in the process of ripping the car apart, they had managed to wipe out, or at least smudge, what fingerprints the guys had left.

All those mistakes. All that carelessness. It was enough to make a guy shudder.

"What a goddamn score that was," I told Zeigler later in Elmhurst.

Zeigler was cautious as hell. "I'm afraid to talk to anybody right now," he said.

I could understand his being worried. The cops had found a telephone number on the chassis of our shortwave radio and had traced it. Now, for chrissake, they knew where everybody went to get their cars souped up and armored. Our favorite garage was about to go out of business.

The papers were screaming the same old stuff about an ordinance should be passed making it legal only for the cops to get bulletproofing and, well, everybody was blaming everybody else.

In Chicago I talked to Freddie. We were all thinking of going back to Reno. First of all, I wanted to get some money in St. Paul. Freddie wanted money too, so I said I'd get $5,000 from Sawyer and a similar amount from Peifer.

The entire operation had made us look pretty goddamn foolish. It had put us in a real bad light. We were never in the habit of talking about scores we pulled, and I didn't expect any criticism from anyone about the Federal Reserve job. I was wrong. I didn't know where the leak was, but everyone seemed to know about the job. And no one could resist sticking the needle in.

"That was a bad caper," Peifer said, when I went to see him in St. Paul.

"What caper?" I bluffed.

"Come off it," Peifer said. "Everybody knows you guys pulled that Reserve Bank job in Chicago. And I want to tell you something. A couple of years ago, some other guys went out on that caper and got just what you got—a bunch of worthless checks. If you'd inquired around, you'd have found it was just no damn good."

Back in Chicago, I told Freddie about this. He was all hot and bothered about Zeigler. "Tell the son of a bitch to think up another caper like that last one," he said.

"It wasn't the guy's fault," I said in Zeigler's defense. "I wish the job had worked out, too, because if there had been as much money in it as Zeigler figured, I'd be in Australia right now."

"Australia?" Freddie was flabbergasted.

"Yeah," I said. "This country is going to get real hot for me. That damn thing with Frank Nash in Kansas City is going to turn out to be the worst thing that ever happened to guys like us. The government will handle bank robberies before long and they're going to scoop everybody up or kill everybody."

Freddie just stood there with his gold teeth showing. But I wasn't kidding. I was smart enough to see the writing on the wall.

"Are you serious about the government and getting scooped up and all that?" he asked.

"Freddie," I said, "we just don't have that much time left."

The Pioneer Press

EDW. G. BREMER KIDNAPED; $200,000 RANSOM ASKED

ABDUCTION VICTIM, KIN AND KIDNAP SQUAD

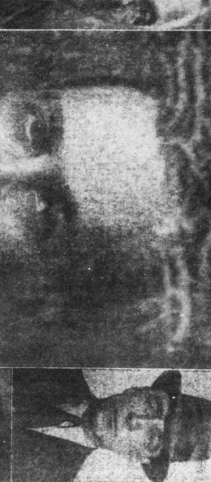

Secrecy Veils Second Major Seizure Here

Victim Member of One of St. Paul's Wealthiest Families; Son of Adolph and Nephew of Otto Bremer, Minnesota Manager of Home Owners Loan Corporation; Phone Call Gave "Tip."

VANISHED AFTER TAKING HIS DAUGHTER TO SUMMIT SCHOOL ON GOODRICH AVENUE

Edward G. Bremer, president of the Commercial State bank and a member of one of St. Paul's wealthiest families, was kidnaped for $200,000 ransom Wednesday morning.

Police say they have received no official notification

12

"So, What the Hell, We Started the Operation Rolling on Our Second Big Kidnapping"

THE KIDNAPPING OF Edward Bremer, president of the Commercial State Bank of St. Paul, in January, 1934, was Harry Sawyer's brainchild, and he was pretty hot on the score. I was a little less than hot on it. For one thing, I figured the feds would move in. For another, an incident way back in 1931 had left me with—well, with some mixed feelings about bankers.

I had loaned my favorite Buick to Phil Courtney. When he didn't tell me exactly why he wanted it, I should have been suspicious, but I wasn't. The next morning I went into McCormick's Restaurant in St. Paul for coffee, and the waitress was acting kind of strange. I had been promising this girl, Louise, that I would take her for a ride in my car, and since she seemed upset, I told her the drive was on.

That did it. She got so goddamn nervous she couldn't hold a cup.

"I wouldn't ride with you for a million dollars," she said.

"What the hell's got into you?" I asked.

"Look," she said, and she shoved an open newspaper in front of me.

Well, Jesus, there it was: a picture of my damn Buick and there was no mistaking it. I'd had a new fender and hubcap put on after a scrape with a taxi and I could see them clearly in the photograph. Then I caught the headline: TWO WOMEN FOUND SLAIN IN BUICK.

One of the women was Indian Rose Walker, who was the widow of Bobby Walker, one of the guys who'd been in on the Denver Mint robbery. He was killed by guards during the caper. The other girl was Marjorie Schwartz. They'd been shot through the head and the car shoved into a snowbank and set on fire. Farmers had put out the blaze.

"Goddamn, you don't think I did that, do you?" I said to Louise.

"Who else? It's your car."

I couldn't convince her and I got sore. "I didn't do it," I said. "And if you ever mention me in connection with this thing, something's going to happen to you."

She got scared then and swore she'd never say a word. I went over to the Green Lantern soon after and told Harry Sawyer the story.

"He shouldn't have left the car there like that," he said. I thought he would have been more upset over those broads getting killed, but he seemed to have other things on his mind.

The rest of the story came out bit by bit. It came from Sawyer himself. It was a weird story, but Sawyer swore it was true. The two women who wound up in my car had set a trap for this banker. The banker had got wind of it and had arranged to have them knocked off.

"That son of a bitch," Sawyer said one day, referring to the banker. "He guaranteed fifty thousand dollars to have those broads killed. And nobody's seen a goddamn cent."

I couldn't figure a guy offering that much money for a couple of easy killings. But that was Sawyer's story. The banker had handled the Denver Mint bonds. Then, when he heard about the girls tailing him, he arranged through Sawyer to have them eliminated.

Sawyer didn't like people who welched, and this guy with the Denver Mint bonds upset him for a long time. Then along came another banker, a man named Edward Bremer, and Sawyer got all worked up again. I don't know what Sawyer's beef was, but he sure didn't like Bremer. And late in 1933, Sawyer began dropping suggestions about my doing something about Bremer.

"I want him grabbed," Sawyer said on several occasions. "It'll run as smooth as the Hamm deal," he said. "I have police contacts. They'll keep me informed. We'll know everything that's happening."

"Forget the cops," I said. "This will be strictly a government thing. We'll have the G to deal with."

"They'll have to prove you took the guy across a state line before they get involved," Sawyer said.

"The government's going to jump right into this, so don't kid yourself about state lines," I said.

I had a sixth sense about these things, but Sawyer kept harping. All we had to do was hold Bremer for a couple of days and we could get $200,000 for our efforts. It sounded good because Freddie and I needed money, but grabbing Bremer wasn't like grabbing Hamm. Bremer was a big name. His old man had put $350,000 into Franklin Roosevelt's 1932 Presidential campaign, and Bremer senior and FDR were pretty close friends. We could expect the feds to go all out to nab the son's kidnappers. All the Bremers were important in St. Paul banking, and the local cops would push hard. The police and the feds had learned a thing or two about catching kidnappers since the Hamm episode, and they'd surely use smarter detection tactics. Everything seemed loaded against us. I told Freddie the heat would be on us like never before.

"Why are we wasting our time talking about heat?" Freddie finally said when he'd heard my arguments once too often. "We've had nothing except heat since 1931."

He was right. So, what the hell, we started the operation rolling on our second big kidnapping.

We lined up the kidnap team—seven guys: Freddie and me, Zeigler, Doc, Bill Weaver, Volney Davis, and Harry Campbell, who had joined us from Oklahoma. We rounded up a place to hold our strategy meetings, an apartment over a beer joint in downtown Chicago. Zeigler looked after the hideout spot where we'd keep Bremer, an old ramshackle house near a freight yard in a town that Zeigler apparently favored as a stowing place for kidnap victims—none other than good old Bensenville, Illinois.

Freddie and I spent some time in St. Paul checking out Bremer and his habits. We hung around the Commercial State Bank long enough to see that he was a big guy, about six feet three and at least two hundred pounds. He was easy enough to spot; he was the guy sitting out in the open behind the desk with the sign on it that read PRESIDENT. He lived with his wife in one of the classy St. Paul residential districts, and everywhere he went, he traveled with a bodyguard.

At first, the bodyguard gave us nervous feelings. The guy was bound to be tough, and he could complicate the actual grab. But, after all, we had seven men and ought to be able to handle one lousy bodyguard. Besides, he'd serve a useful purpose after the grab. He could act as messenger boy, carrying the ransom notes and money back and forth between us and Bremer's family.

Bremer followed a strict routine every morning. At about eight thirty he left his house and drove his little daughter to a private school. Then he headed downtown and parked in a garage near the bank. His bodyguard met him there, and together they walked through a small park to the bank building.

The grab, we figured, would come in the park. It was reasonably secluded, a spot where a few men meeting together apparently on the way to work wouldn't attract any special notice. We planned to wait nearby in a couple of cars, intercept Bremer and his bodyguard as they entered the park, hustle them quietly and quickly into one of our cars, and beat it in a hurry.

While we were waiting to put the plan into operation, though, a couple of things happened. We had the guns stored in some suitcases in the apartment that Freddie and Ma were sharing, but all of them needed cleaning and checking. All right, we'd get Ma out of the apartment and oil up the guns, but then where the hell would they be safe?

I came up with a great solution. I bought a jukebox from a guy, unscrewed the big front section where the speakers sat, took out the speakers, and slid the guns into the empty space. The machine still played, and I told Dolores I was bringing home a record player for her. She was really excited, but when I walked in with the jukebox she blew her top. She told me I was turning our apartment into a pool hall.

The other incident was a lot more serious. It happened because Freddie and I thought the cops were tailing us. We were sitting around an apartment in St. Paul where Bill Weaver lived with a shoplifter named Myrtle Eaton, when someone noticed a guy peeping through the window of an apartment across the alley. We took a look outside and spotted a car with two guys who looked like cops. We pulled out and drove back to my apartment.

Later we went back and found the cops still there. We gave them a careful look and once again drove away in our car. The two cops followed us. Freddie was at the wheel, and I told him to pull around a corner and stop suddenly. He did, and I leaped out of the passenger side with a machine gun. I must have thrown twenty or thirty slugs into the cop car. When we drove away that time, nobody was trailing us.

I'd made a bad mistake. The next day the story was in the papers. The guys I took for cops worked at the St. Paul airport. Their caps just made them look like cops. One of them lived in the apartment across the alley from Weaver. His wife had called him at work to tell him a peeping tom was bothering her. He drove home with a buddy from work and parked outside to catch the peeper. And all they caught were some bullets. Luckily neither of them died, though I did hit one guy in the liver and he was in pretty rough shape.

The job was spooked. The whole deal looked like one giant-sized jinx, and the situation got worse a couple of days before the grab when Harry Sawyer told us that Bremer had suddenly fired his bodyguard. We made a quick revision of the overall plan and decided to snatch Bremer before he reached downtown. We'd take him out of his car just after he dropped his kid at school. A couple of blocks from the school, he'd have to pull up for a stop sign at a street named Lexington. That was the spot where we'd move in. I didn't like the idea of changing the plan on such short notice, but on the morning of January 19, 1934, we went into action.

We used two cars. Zeigler and Freddie in one car pulled in front of Bremer at Lexington, blocking his way. Doc and Volney Davis swung out of the back seat of the car I was driving behind Bremer and moved to either side of Bremer's car. The idea was for them to ease Bremer quickly into the back seat and wheel off in his car. But as I watched, a wild scuffle suddenly broke out. Bremer was trying to get away. I saw Doc pull out his pistol and smack Bremer on the head. Doc and Davis shoved him onto the floor at the back. Then, at last, we all pulled away in a fleet of three cars.

We drove to a rendezvous in the country outside St. Paul. Zeigler had prepared three ransom notes addressed to Bremer's father. We needed Bremer's signature, but he had trouble concentrating on the job. He was bleeding like a stuck pig where Doc had slugged him. When he'd finally signed, we blindfolded him and switched him into my car for the drive to Bensenville. We left his car in a field. Zeigler and Freddie headed back into St. Paul to deliver the notes, and the rest of us set out for the hideout and the wait for the ransom money.

It turned out to be a long, grueling wait. Bremer wasn't exactly the model prisoner Hamm had been. The wound in his head didn't help his disposition, but even apart from it, he was just naturally a slightly miserable bastard. And it was my job to tend to most of the guard duties. I had my fill of Edward Bremer.

On the first night, I led him into the room we had prepared for him, a room with boarded-up windows, and he started in objecting. I bandaged his wound, and he demanded a drink. I didn't have any booze. I got him coffee. He asked how much ransom we wanted. I told him $200,000, and he let out a yell. "You're crazy," he said. "My father wouldn't pay that much for me." I could believe it.

Next day, he started whining about his watch—a beautiful piece of jewelry studded with rubies. Bremer said it had been a gift from his poor dead mother. It was a precious keepsake and he didn't want to lose it. I told him we hadn't the faintest intention of stealing his damned watch.

Next it was a train receipt in his wallet. Please don't use it as an identification for me, Bremer said. The receipt showed that two people had traveled in a drawing room from St. Paul to Chicago. And Bremer's wife thought he'd made the trip to Chicago alone.

Bremer hardly ever let up. At one point, he told me that we had kidnapped the wrong man. He said that he knew a man in St. Paul who had put aside a quarter of a million dollars in a safety deposit box to be used by the guy's wife in case he should ever be kidnapped. Bremer told me that we should have grabbed that guy instead. He was suggesting it would have been an easier ransom situation.

He intimated that, anyway, all I had to do was contact him sometime after his father had ransomed him and that he and I could get together on some lucrative deals. He said that he was a good buddy of Harry Sawyer's and of Jack Peifer's and that either guy would vouch for him. The mention of Sawyer and Peifer surprised me a little at first, but I didn't pursue the matter. Maybe Bremer did know them. After all, Sawyer and Peifer were pretty well known people around the Twin Cities. In any case, I really didn't want to get involved.

Meanwhile, in the outside world, the Bremer kidnapping was stirring up nothing but trouble and confusion. When the cops found Bremer's car, they looked at the blood his wound had spread all over the floor and upholstery and drew the brilliant conclusion that he was dead. They had guys from the police department, the fire department, the American Legion, and the Boy Scouts out digging in the field where we'd left the car. They figured Bremer's body was buried there.

They got some support for their theory when a screwball wrote to the Bremer family claiming that he was in on the kidnapping—that he and the other kidnappers had killed Bremer and buried his body in a snowbank near Anoka, Minnesota. His letter set the cops off on another round of digging.

President Roosevelt even mentioned the kidnapping in one of his fireside chats on the radio. He, too, went on the assumption that his friend's son was killed, and he swore that the feds would capture the killers. The FBI, partly with Roosevelt's encouragement, descended on St. Paul in droves. They raided every joint in town and questioned every hood. They even called Jack Peifer in for grilling—and Peifer was all the way down in Hot Springs. He'd gone to the baths to take treatments for syphilis.

All the action made it tough for Freddie and Zeigler to deal for the ransom, and Bremer's old man made it a lot tougher. He tried to negotiate the sum down to $100,000. Freddie and Zeigler stuck to the original $200,000. The old man came back with a demand for proof that his son was still alive. We ordered Bremer to write a couple of letters, one to his father, the other to his wife.

Ten days went by, twelve days, and all of us in Bensenville were getting twitchy. Bill Weaver developed something like claustrophobia. Bremer got more irritating by the minute. The whole deal was getting me down.

Zeigler said that he wasn't having much trouble communicating with old man Bremer, but that the FBI were intercepting all of Bremer senior's moves. He said that he figured he'd get away from St. Paul for a couple of days and take care of some other private business. Zeigler disappeared, and next day I read in the paper that one of the Syndicate guys who had questioned me about the Touhy Gang, Willie White, was found in Oak Park, Illinois, shot through the head. I decided that Zeigler had handled an execution job. He was a cool operator.

Twenty days from the moment we grabbed Bremer, Zeigler and Freddie arrived with two suit boxes. We counted out $200,000 in used bills. We had our ransom.

We also had a note from old man Bremer. He addressed us as "sports," which struck me as a strange name for the kidnappers of his son, and he asked us to live up to our end of the bargain as he had lived up to his. He pointed out that all the bills were marked. The FBI had recorded the serial number of each and every one. But old man Bremer asked us not to hold the marking against him. The FBI had forced him to agree to it.

We had no intention of laying a finger on Bremer. I personally was only too anxious to get rid of him, but not with a gun. Again I was in charge of the release, and I planned to let Bremer out in Rochester, Minnesota. But first I made a few preparations. I went out to a store and bought him a new set of clothes, everything from underwear to a suit. I burned all of his old clothes, and I ordered Doc and Harry

Campbell, who were accompanying me to Rochester, to put on gloves and not to take them off until we had dropped Bremer. I'd heard that the FBI now had techniques that would lift prints even from clothes.

On the drive to Rochester, Bremer was his customary complaining self. He objected to the blindfold we put on him and, of all things, he kept bringing up his garters. I'd burned them along with all his other stuff, and he whined that they were the best garters he'd ever owned. He bitched, too, about the police. How the hell, he said, could he have been held prisoner for twenty days without the cops turning him up? Bremer had a point.

He was still beefing when I pulled up the car around the corner from the railway depot in Rochester. "All right, Bremer," I said, "beat it." He did, and so did we. I drove all out to Chicago.

All of us kidnappers met a couple of days later to divide up the loot. It was in fives and tens, and each one of us counted out $25,000. The remaining $25,000 was split between Harry Sawyer and Chuck Fitzgerald, who was still mending from his South St. Paul Post Office job wounds.

The money felt good to touch, but a problem still hung over us—how the hell were we going to spend it? It was hot. The FBI had marked it, and they'd soon enough round up anyone who passed the stuff. We decided to discount it with the same two Reno guys who'd taken the Hamm money.

Doc carried the money out to Reno and flew back with a big fat zero. Nobody wanted to touch it. It was too damned hot. But the Reno guys had been generous. They gave Doc seven thousand-dollar bills to distribute among the kidnappers. It was a nice thought.

I wasn't in a panic about the Bremer money, though. I was confident I could spend it at some point. But at the same time, it was like a damned albatross around my neck. The kidnapping had the FBI plenty excited. They were determined to pin it on somebody, and stories appeared in the Chicago papers speculating that the Karpis-Barker Gang might be mixed up in the snatch. As long as I was walking around with the ransom money, it would be easy enough for the feds to nail me for the job—*if* they could lay their hands on me.

I didn't like it. I wished I'd never heard of the caper. I wished, most of all, I'd never loaned my car to Phil Courtney, the guy who'd knocked off the two girls. It was that damned Buick of mine that got me into the mess.

ROSEN KEYNOTE CITES ECONOMY IN PUBLIC WORK

Politics Eliminated and Better Service Given, Commissioner Says.

KING OPENS MAYOR DRIVE

Other Candidates Reiterate Charges and Pledges at Rallies.

Politics has been eliminated from the city department of public works. Commissioner Milton Rosen said in his opening campaign rally Tuesday night, and 425 miles of dirt streets have been scarified at a reduced cost because of a new method of treatment adopted.

About 3,000 persons crowded the Marquette room and corridors of the Ryan hotel for the rally, which with the opening of his campaign for mayor by Dr. George L. King, featured Tuesday's developments in the city election campaign.

Other developments included:

E. M. O'Neill, former city councilman, spoke for Mayor Bundlie in a radio address, and asserted that badly in Mr. Bundlie's administration cost the city a reduced car company taxes.

Harry N. Peterson, former county attorney, spoke in behalf of William Mahoney, candidate for mayor, and continued Mr. Mahoney's attack on Mayor Bundlie.

Mayor Bundlie at three meetings reiterated his program of tax reduction and his assertion that his opponents have no definite program.

John J. Courtney, candidate for mayor, asserted that the schools the five paid police departments are the most important functions of the city government, and announced his intention to move to cut the budget of the first year of his administration, to aid in a further reduction.

ROOSEVELT WINS BIG VICTORY IN N. H. VOTE

Lead Over Smith 4,500 With Only 60 of 294 Precincts Missing

Concord, N. H., March 9.—(Wednesday)—Candidates pledged to the support of Franklin D. Roosevelt for the Democratic presidential nomination won a sweeping victory over the forces backing Alfred E. Smith in today's New Hampshire primary, first of the national campaign.

With 80 scattering towns and city wards of the 294 in the state missing, the returns of the vote for delegates at large to the Democratic national convention showed an average majority for the eight Roosevelt pledged candidates of approximately 4,500 over that for the eight Smith pledged candidates.

The vote for candidates for district

Second of Slain Women Tentatively Identified as Up-State Crime Figure

Believed Recent Jailmate of Other; Chief Brown Investigates Secretly.

The second of two women murdered and burned Saturday night near Turtle Lake, Wis., was tentatively identified Tuesday as Marjorie Schwarts, 27 years old, of Virginia, Minn., recent jailmate of the other woman, Mrs. Margaret Perry, alias "Indian Rose," Denver mint robbery figure.

The tentative identification was made by Chief of Detectives Robert Donaldson of Duluth, who said Miss Schwarts was discharged from the St. Louis county work farm simultaneously with Mrs. Perry.

Three investigations of the crime are under way. One is being conducted by Wisconsin authorities, including the fire marshal and Polk county officers. A second is in charge of police of Duluth and Superior.

Chief Donaldson said the Schwarts woman is well known to police in Duluth and on the Iron Range. Credence was lent to the identification by the fact that in St. Paul the slain pair registered as "Margaret and Marjorie Perry," using the true first names of both and the true last name of one. In Minneapolis, where they registered at the Elgin hotel Saturday for a room they never occupied, they registered as "Marjorie Perry and Clara White."

The third investigation, centering in St. Paul, is proceeding secretly under the direction of Chief of Police Thomas A. Brown. Developments are expected from it, but no intimation is obtainable as to what their nature will be.

The names of three St. Paul men have entered the case. Tom and James Filben, are partners in the Patrick Novelty Co., and were sought unsuccessfully recently as witnesses before a Ramsey county grand jury investigating slot machine rackets here.

The third is Jack Peiffer, erstwhile minor tax defendant and former

(Please Turn to Page 2, Col. 2.)

Victim, Ex-mate

MARGARET PERRY.

BOBBY WALKER.

One of the two women found burned Saturday night near Turtle Lake, Wis., was tentatively identified as Margaret Perry, alias "Indian Rose." She is said to have been the common law wife of "Denver Bobby" Walker, wanted in connection with the Denver mint robbery ten years ago. The other victim was identified tentatively as Marjorie Schwarts of Virginia, a recent jailmate of Margaret Perry in St. Louis county.

FLOWERS CONVICTED IN BANK FRAUD CASE

Found Guilty of Permitting Excessive Loans From Institution Now Defunct.

Le Center, Minn., March 8.—H. H. Flowers, former secretary of the Minnesota Rural Credit bureau, was convicted by a Le Sueur county jury tonight on a charge of permitting and approving excessive loans from the Cleveland State bank, of which he was vice president. The bank since has been closed.

Sentence will be pronounced Wednesday by Judge Albert H. Enersen. The jury's verdict was returned less than twelve hours after presentation of testimony was begun this morning. The jury deliberated three hours and twenty minutes.

Flowers who faces a sentence of one year in jail, a $1,000 fine, or both, served three months in the St. Paul workhouse last year, after he pleaded guilty to benefiting from a trans-

DEFINITE PROGRESS RETURN OF CHILD R... AT FAMOUS FLIER...

Police Trace Ladder Used in Kidn... Sold by N. J. Epileptic Home and i... in Hopewell Area; Servants Had... Time of Abduction, Investigators

INCREASING INTEREST SHOWN... OF PARENTS TO DEAL DIREC...

Hopewell, N. J., March 8.—(AP)—Definite pro... tonight toward returning the kidnaped Charles Jr. to the home of his famous parents.

This news came from the Sourland mounta... after a close friend of Colonel Lindbergh had lef...

The encouraging word—the first of its kin... hilltop home since the child was stolen a we... telephoned to state police at Trenton in respo... the night press conference there.

"What are the latest developments in the... What are the latest developments in Colonel... separate investigation?"

"Progress," was the single word answer ma... by Major Charles Schoeffel of the state police.

Earlier the New York Daily News related... sation with a member of the Lindbergh househ... noon:

"Has any progress been made?"

"We have not made any headway in ident... but we are more hopeful for the return of th... two letters were received. That is all I can say."

Finally it was learned there had been a... the corps of state police stationed at the Li... incoming mail previously was freed of any su... sorship, as were telegraphic and telephonic co...

Whether the next step would be complet... thorities themselves was conjectural. Governor... offered to take such action should the Colonel...

Meanwhile, although state police denied... identification of the ladder used by the kidn... the wood of which the ladder was constructed... lumber sold by the Skillman (N. J.) State Ho...

The ladder is one of the few definite clue... It was used to gain entrance to the nursery... stolen a week ago tonight and was found abo...

Anderson Wins Race for Mayor Of Alexandria

Two Incumbents Defeated for Alderman in Rochester Election.

Alexandria, Minn., March 8.—Carl V. Anderson was re-elected mayor of Alexandria, Minn., today, defeating A. J. Du Bueau by a vote of 1,140 to 421.

GAS SERVICE VOTED.

Austin, Minn., March 8.—Voters authorized a charter amendment authorizing the city of Austin to engage in distribution of natural gas. A zoning law also was approved. An amendment to make the city assessor an appointive instead of elective officer also was defeated.

INCUMBENTS DEFEATED.

Rochester, Minn., March 8.—Two incumbents were defeated in Rochester's charter election complete unofficial returns showed tonight.

John M. Norton defeated Henry F. Vitstedt, incumbent, 442 to 430, for Second ward alderman and Paul H. Dallmon was re-elected Third ward alderman over O. W. Schroeder, 466 to 443.

The only woman candidate, Miss Ethel Oesterreich, was elected Third

greatwoman to uerque Man in o Springs

Lake Michigan Vessels Held at Storm's Mercy

Several Unreported as Belated Winter Unlooses Fury.

HOUSES WASHED AWAY.

Manteo, N. C., March 8.—(AP)—At Avon, in the southern end of Hatteras, except three, have been washed away, a message from the reaching here tonight said...

13

"On the Run"

SHOTGUN GEORGE ZEIGLER died on the street in front of Sargeant's Restaurant in Cicero, Illinois. He had stepped out of the restaurant late one night and crossed Twenty-second Street to his car. He was alone, and he was just putting the key into the door on the driver's side of the car, when someone called to him from behind. "Hey, George." Zeigler turned, and the guy who called, whoever he was, leveled Zeigler with a blast of buckshot. Zeigler never knew what hit him.

The killing came a couple of months after the Bremer kidnapping, and Doc figured that it was a Syndicate job, a deliberate rubout to keep Zeigler from talking. Zeigler had been getting kind of gabby about the job and about a lot of other things, too, and the Syndicate knew that if he were

173

picked up by the FBI, he might open up and reveal information on Syndicate-ordered executions. As it was, even in death, Zeigler brought a touch of danger to all of us kidnappers. When the FBI searched his body, they found the thousand-dollar bill from the two guys in Reno, and the feds traced it to the Federal Reserve Bank in San Francisco. It could have been only a matter of time, we suspected, until they checked it and the other bills through to Chicago and, maybe, right to us.

We'd had enough of Chicago. It was time for Freddie and me to hit the road. We packed up our Bremer money and, leaving Ma Barker in a Chicago apartment, we moved to Toledo. We were hardly lonely over there. I took Dolores with me, Freddie had Paula the drunk, and Doc, Harry Campbell, and Bill Weaver all followed us into Ohio. Toledo felt just like home.

Doc Barker made a trip back to Chicago and spent a few days moving from store to store changing some of the ransom money. It was easy to do, since the cash was all in fives and tens. Doc unloaded $25,000 worth of the hot stuff.

He also peddled $10,000 at a ten percent discount to a guy in Chicago named Boss McLaughlin. The rest of us agreed with Doc to let McLaughlin have the money on an experimental basis. If he passed $10,000 without stirring up any fuss, we'd sell him more of the ransom. But McLaughlin bungled the job. Only a few days after Doc made the delivery, the FBI picked up McLaughlin and two other guys on suspicion of dealing in unlawful currency.

Toledo turned out to be an unhappy town for us. We were low on money. We fell into a lot of nasty bickering. A couple of people started drinking too much. Freddie's girl, Paula, was the worst boozer of all and her habits caused a lot of friction. We were all frustrated over the Bremer situation. We had the cash, but we couldn't spend it.

It didn't improve relations when I was offered a job in Cleveland and Freddie wasn't. He didn't care for the snub. The offer came from the two guys who ran the Harvard Club. They were being harassed by a rival organization in the city. The owners needed a handy gun to keep the opposition in line, and they came to me with a good proposition. I took it.

I worked around the club's offices, learning as much as I could about the operation. I used to oversee part of the gambling business. I checked the dice every day to be certain they were honest. I kept an eye on the safe. On a good weekend it held up to a quarter of a million dollars.

But my principal concern was to keep tabs on the rival outfit. I made a list of the names and addresses of all the guys who worked for the opposition. Then I drove around to each one of their houses and made a long, detailed note on the physical layouts of the homes, the families who lived in them and their habits. But I didn't stop there. I handed a copy of my files to a middleman and instructed him to deliver it to the boss of the opposition, with a warning. If there was any trouble, I said, any hint of an attempt to shake down the Harvard Club, then he could expect me to knock off all the guys in my files, rough up their kids, and burn down their houses.

The Harvard Club owners liked my thoroughness, and showed their appreciation. They cut me in for two and a half percent of the profits and provided Dolores and me with a bungalow in a pleasant part of Cleveland. Dolores was glad to settle in since she was pregnant, that second pregnancy.

From time to time, to keep us from forgetting just how constant the heat really was, an incident would come along to scare the hell out of us. There was, for instance, the issue of *Liberty* magazine in the spring of '34. It ran large pictures of Pretty Boy Floyd, Baby Face Nelson, Doc Barker, Freddie, and me, and it offered a $5,000 reward to any man who brought us in dead. The story called us "mad dogs," and it made a big point of underlining the fact that it would pay no reward if we were taken alive.

Not long after, Freddie and I drove to Chicago to visit Ma. We took her to a movie and a special announcement was flashed on the screen. "These men are public enemies," it read. And then came the pictures—John Dillinger, Baby Face Nelson, Doc, Freddie, and me. The punch line was, "Remember, one of these men may be sitting beside you."

The lights went on in the theater. The audience looked around and giggled. They didn't believe that any public enemies could ever be sitting beside them. Freddie and I knew better. So did Ma. She had just got the first real confirmation that her boys were more than ordinary crooks.

Another low point came one night in July when Dolores and I dropped around to a neighborhood Cleveland theater to see a movie called *Manhattan Melodrama*. I didn't particularly care for the ending—a guy on his way to the electric chair. But that didn't bother me half as much as the words I heard as we came out of the theater.

A kid selling newspapers was shouting, "Dillinger shot."

I bought a paper and read the gory details. Dillinger had also gone to a movie that night, to the Biograph Theater on North Clark Street in Chicago. He had a couple of broads with him, and when he walked out of the theater, the FBI shot him down in the street.

A few days later, the papers brought more bad news. The cops had gunned down Dillinger's longtime friend Homer Van Meter in St. Paul.

Freddie and I decided that we'd better think about moving and that we'd better unload the Bremer money. While we were scouting around for a market, we buried the hot cash— almost $100,000, representing a partial share from Freddie, me, Doc, Bill Weaver, and Volney Davis—in a hole in the garage attached to my bungalow.

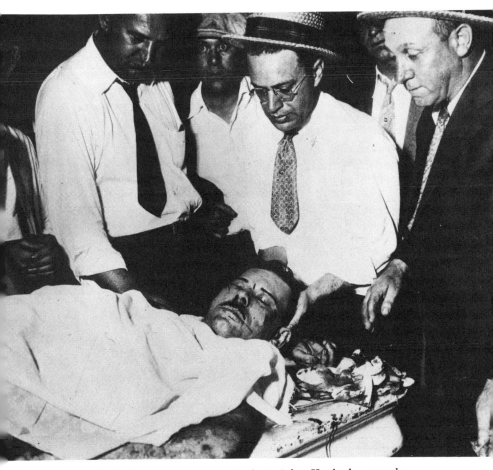

"Dillinger had also gone to a movie that night. He had a couple of broads with him, and when he walked out of the theater, the FBI shot him down in the street." — **UPI**

We made contact with a rich hood in Grosse Point, Michigan, who came up with a good scheme for peddling the money. It would cost us fifteen percent, but we liked his plan to unload it in Cuba. He could guarantee that the hot bills wouldn't turn up in Havana but in safer places like Caracas and Mexico City.

We agreed to the deal, and Freddie and I went home to dig up the money. We had buried it in a couple of leather cases, and when we pulled them out of the ground, the bills were soaking wet. The leather had let through the moisture. The bills looked like they'd been floating in a lake, and we had a hell of a time drying them, especially since we had waited until a few hours before our man was due to leave for Cuba to dig it out of the ground.

We worked like madmen. First we tried rocking the stuff around in a washing machine. Then we sent Dolores out to buy a couple of electric fans. We laid the bills out on the living-room floor, placed a fan at either end of the room, and turned them on. We had a hell of a time keeping the bills from floating up to the ceiling. But eventually we got them in shape. They weren't exactly crisp. Still they didn't drip every time you squeezed them. And the acid test came in Cuba, when our contact from Grosse Point had no trouble selling the money, even if it was slightly soggy. We were back in the chips.

We left Cleveland abruptly on the night of the day Freddie's girl, Paula, got drunk with a couple of other broads in a bar, so drunk that the cops arrested her and started checking into her contacts. It didn't take them long to pin her down and start after Freddie and me. The feds didn't know how close they were to nailing us. They almost had us that night in Cleveland.

Freddie, Doc, and Harry Campbell came knocking on the door of my bungalow in the dead of the night. We decided to clear out immediately, but there were machine guns in the house that Freddie and Paula had been living in and in the rooms Doc and Campbell shared. We decided to scout the house and apartment and rescue the guns if the coast was clear.

We drove first to Freddie's. No sign of the cops. We hustled the guns out of the house. We drove to Campbell's apartment. It looked safe enough. Freddie, Doc, and Campbell hopped out of the car and started across the street to the building. A light went on in the front room of the apartment. The three guys froze in the street. The light stayed on for thirty seconds, and we could see men's shadows moving. Some dumb cop's goof up there had saved us. We jumped back in the car and beat it.

We decided, however, to carry our investigation of Harry and Doc's apartment another step. We sent a friend of ours named Josh around, carrying a check with him signed with the alias that Campbell had used to rent the apartment. He was to tell the guys who answered the door that the tenant had given him a bum check and he was looking to collect his debt.

Josh carried out his act perfectly.

"Goddamn," he said when he got back, "they got shotguns and pistols and everything in there. They really grabbed me when I knocked on that door. They roughed me around. But those guys aren't city police. Those are feds."

We took another drive past Freddie's house and spotted six cars parked in a row outside the building, with four or five men in each one. We drove to my bungalow. The two guys I was working for at the Harvard Club arrived and told us that it'd be best if we cleared out of Cleveland. We didn't need their advice. We were already leaving.

We drove to Toledo, then on to Chicago. I was hot. Dolores was pregnant. We had to keep moving. I liked the sound of Cuba. I told Freddie that I wanted to get Dolores away, and I set out with her by car for Miami. I packed my bags with care for the trip—a machine gun, several clips of ammunition, and two bulletproof vests.

In Miami I got in touch with a contact named Joe Adams. He agreed to store my guns and equipment at the Biscayne Kennel Club, a dog track that he owned a piece of, and he took my car off my hands. It didn't seem to matter to him that the FBI probably had the license number. I thanked him and caught a boat out of Key West for Havana.

Dolores and I settled into Veradero, a summer resort where the Cuban President spent his holidays and where American millionaires went to get away from it all. I made a useful contact with a guy named Nate Heller, who owned the Parkview Hotel in Havana and seemed to know everything that was going on among the U.S. gangsters hiding out in Cuba. Heller, I decided, would make a good information pipeline.

But I was still haunted by things from back home. One time I was sitting in the American Bar in Havana talking to the bartender's wife. She was leafing through a copy of *Famous Detective Story Magazine,* and she flipped it open to a picture. It was a photograph of me.

"If I didn't know better," she said, "I'd swear that was you."

"Yeah," I said, "I suppose there is a resemblance."

Another night, Doroles and I were listening to the Lowell Thomas newscast. He said FBI men had found Pretty Boy Floyd. They'd shot it out with him on a farm in Ohio. Floyd was dead.

The last time I had seen Floyd was a few months earlier in the parking lot of the Harvard Club. He and Adam Richette had driven up in a new Ford coupe and sent somebody to get me. They felt safer in the car. Both men were wanted by the FBI for complicity in the Union Station Massacre in Kansas City, and I wasn't too happy about them knowing where I was. Adam hadn't taken part in the massacre, but the FBI didn't know this and he was just as hot over this caper as he would have been had he actually been on it.

Pretty Boy Floyd wanted to get in with us guys. And so did Adam. But there wasn't a chance. We had enough troubles of our own. We parted on good terms, though, and they said that if we ever needed them, they could be contacted through a guy named Jumbo Crowley in Canton, Ohio.

That radio announcement ended any thoughts we might have had of including those guys in on anything.

That was in October of '34 and, a couple of weeks later, Lowell Thomas came on with more crime news. This time it was about Baby Face Nelson. Someone had spotted him

"Pretty Boy Floyd wanted to get in with us guys. But there wasn't a chance. We had enough troubles of our own." — UPI

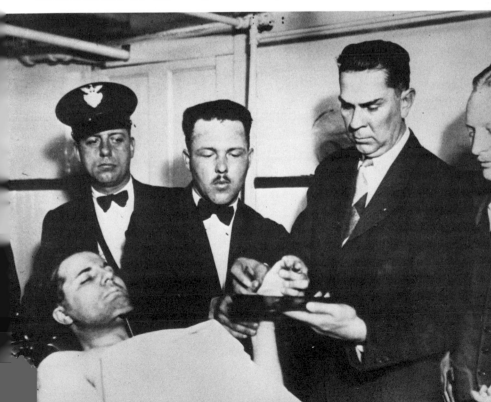

driving down a street in a suburb of Chicago. The G-men arrived. Everybody started shooting. Nelson killed two of the FBI guys. The rest of the agents got him. He was dead, too. *The cops were knocking off all the big crooks.*

One afternoon I took a $1,000 bill to the Royal Bank of Canada on the Prado in Havana and asked for $750 in tens and $250 in fives. The teller gave me my money, and some of the bills were discolored. I checked them over at the hotel and recognized them as bills that I'd buried in the garage back in Cleveland. The big shot from Grosse Point, Michigan, had been stringing us a line. His guarantee that the Bremer money would go to Caracas and Mexico City was a pack of lies. The money was in Havana and, sooner or later it was bound to attract the feds.

Then one day I was standing in the lobby of the Parkview Hotel when a brisk guy, obviously an American, walked up to the desk. I watched him fill in a registration card. He gave his name as Kingman and his home Jacksonville, Florida. I didn't trust his looks.

At dinner that very night Nate Heller told me that an FBI agent had just arrived from Florida. He was looking for Bremer's kidnappers. Some of the ransom money had turned up in Havana, and the feds were certain the guys responsible for the job were on the island. Heller said the agent had pulled out a picture and shown it to him. It was a picture of me.

I asked Heller what the FBI agent's name was.

Kingman.

I always could sniff out a fed.

It was time to check out of Cuba. Dolores was happy. We'd be back in the U.S.A. for Christmas. Freddie and Ma were renting a cottage at Lake Weir in northern Florida, and Harry Campbell and his girl, Wynona, were visiting them for a few weeks. It'd be old home week for all of us.

Dolores and I reached Florida without any trouble from

Kingman. My Miami friend Joe Adams got me a house in the Miami suburb of Little River and arranged for me to buy a brand-new 1935 Buick Special.

It was great to see Freddie again. We talked about our favorite topic—planning robberies. At one point, we decided to drive up to Cleveland to look into the possibilities of work. We got together with Doc Barker in Cleveland. He'd come over from Chicago, and we set up a score that looked promising for sometime later in the winter. There we heard a funny story about the aftermath of our fast escape from Cleveland back in the fall.

The story came from Frank Noonan, the guy who ran the private detective agency and who was a pal of the U.S. Attorney General's. It seemed that when I beat it out of my Cleveland bungalow, I had left behind some payroll envelopes that came from Noonan's agency. An FBI man named Cowley came around to question Noonan about the envelopes and wasn't satisfied with his answers. He told Noonan that he was convinced there was a criminal connection between me and the agency. Cowley said that he had to go to Chicago for a couple of days but that when he returned, he'd give Noonan a tough time. Cowley never made it back from Chicago. He was one of the two agents Baby Face Nelson killed in the shoot-out.

From Cleveland we drove to Freddie's place at Lake Weir. It was a gorgeous layout. The cottage sat fifty yards from the lake, and it came with a boathouse and a launch. A stone fence, about waist-high, surrounded the property, and the grounds were crowded with grapefruit, orange, and lemon trees. It was a small paradise, and Ma had the luxury of a maid and a gardener.

I stayed with the Barkers for a few days. Harry Campbell and Wynona were there, and we put in some wonderful hours fishing. Campbell was the guy who supplied most of the

"Campbell was the guy who supplied most of the laughs — and a lot of the nervous moments as well. He was a wild man." — UPI

laughs—and a lot of the nervous moments as well. He was a wild man.

Earlier during our Florida stay, he'd almost put us all in a jackpot. Harry had a bad habit of driving when he was drunk, and one day he was barreling along a Florida highway, completely plastered, when he smashed into an old Model T Ford. The accident wasn't entirely Harry's fault. The Model T had run through a stop sign. But Harry was drunk and, besides, a young guy and his wife were killed in the other car. They had a baby with them and, by some miracle, it survived the crash.

The sheriff from the nearest small town slammed Harry into jail and, when he sobered up, he realized that he was in a hot situation. If the sheriff took his fingerprints and sent them to Washington, the FBI would descend on Harry and the rest of us. Harry used his head. He worked a deal with the sheriff. He said he'd need a new car. He suggested that maybe he'd buy it in the sheriff's town. The sheriff told Harry, just by coincidence, that one of his best friends happened to be the local Ford dealer. Well, the upshot was that Harry bought a new Ford, donated $250 toward the care of the baby, and, in return, the sheriff bade him a friendly good-bye.

When I decided I had to get back to Dolores, Ma was sorry to have me go. I'd never seen her so mellow. She told me to phone her as soon as Dolores' baby was born. She said she'd come down to our place and look after things, help out while Dolores was busy with the baby. I couldn't believe my ears. Ma was the one who never liked our women. She hadn't shown much warmth to Dolores in the past, but she seemed a changed woman at Lake Weir. When I pulled away from the place by the lake, I was looking forward to seeing Ma down at our house, helping out, taking care of Dolores and our kid.

Harry and Wynona drove with me down to my place at

"If the FBI got Ma and Freddie, then they might get me and Dolores and Harry and Wynona next."
Wynona Burdette after capture in the hotel raid in Atlantic City
— UPI

Little River. We checked in with Dolores, and Harry and I, leaving Wynona to keep Dolores company, drove farther south for a little sport. We fished in the Gulf Stream, in Biscayne Bay, and off Everglades City where the trolling for mackerel was terrific. The morning came when Harry had planned to drive back to Lake Weir, but he told Wynona that he felt like one more day of fishing. I took him over for a last crack at the mackerel. We put in a full day, and it was almost dark by the time we took our boat, loaded with fish, into the dock.

We drove to Little River, and at nine thirty we swung onto Eighty-fourth Street. I saw a car parked about a block from my place. Dolores and Wynona were sitting in the front seat. I pulled over to the curb. Dolores ran over to my car.

"You should have come home sooner," she said. She was nearly hysterical.

"Take it easy," I said. "Tell me what's the matter."

She took a lot of deep breaths.

"The FBI shot up Freddie and Ma's place," she said.

She stopped.

"Freddie's dead. Ma's dead."

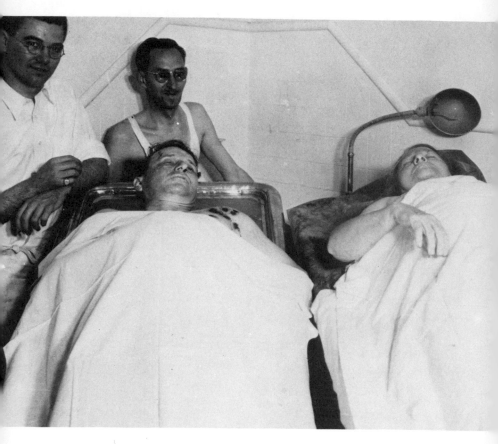

"*I felt two emotions when Dolores told me about Freddie and Ma: Grief and fear. I was torn up that Ma and Freddie were dead. Freddie was my best friend. Ma was like a mother.*"
— WIDE WORLD PHOTOS

14

"Freddie and Ma Were Gone.
But We Were Still Free and Loose"

I FELT TWO EMOTIONS when Dolores told me about Freddie and Ma: grief and fear. I was torn up that Ma and Freddie were dead. Freddie was my best friend. Ma was like a mother. I'd lived through a lot with both of them. But I was scared too. If the FBI got them, then they might get me and Dolores and Harry and Wynona next. I had to keep cool. Freddie and Ma were gone, but we were still free and loose.

Dolores had first heard that the Barkers and the rest of us were in trouble when she'd taken a phone call for me earlier in the day. The call was a tipoff from the underworld. It came from Cleveland, warning us all to get out of our houses before nightfall. Dolores didn't know whether Freddie had got the same call. She wasn't even sure who the warning came from. All she knew was what she'd heard later on the radio. The FBI moved in on Freddie and Ma at Lake Weir. They went at the house shooting, and they mowed the Barkers down.

We weren't going to wait around. I took Dolores, Harry, and Wynona straight to Joe Adams' place in Miami. There I picked up $1,000 and worked out a plan. Harry and I would put the two girls on a train that night for Atlantic City and the two of us would drive north in my new Buick Special. The meeting place for the girls and us was to be the Danmore Hotel, a place in Atlantic City that one of Joe Adams' boys recommended.

Harry and I said good-bye to the girls outside the station and aimed north. We drove all night and all the next day, skirting the big cities. Finally, we arrived at the Danmore Hotel in Atlantic City.

Dolores and Wynona had made it safely to the hotel, but the next day I wasn't so sure that there was anything safe about Atlantic City. I figured I was being followed. Harry thought the same thing. I took Dolores to a doctor for a checkup. She was well into her eighth month. I picked up some clothes to replace my summer stuff from Florida and had my hair trimmed. And all the time I sensed I was being tailed. I spotted a man and a woman, both in their forties, who seemed to be sticking behind me through all my travels around the city.

I talked the situation over with Harry. He said he'd picked out a couple of people on *his* tail. We agreed to move. We'd sleep in the Danmore one more night, then head for New York City. We told the girls to pack for an early morning checkout and got into bed before midnight, Dolores and me in a front room on the third floor, Wynona and Harry in a room down the hall.

Somebody knocked on my door around daybreak. I got up in my underwear and opened the door a crack. It was Mrs. Morley, who ran the hotel with her husband. She said there were five detectives downstairs. They were looking for Harry and me, but they didn't know what rooms we were sleeping in. Mrs. Morley had come up to warn us—or so she said.

"Why don't you hide under the bed in one of those empty rooms down the hall?" she said.

I heard the floor squeak in the second-floor hall. I looked over the banister. Three plainclothesmen were moving quietly down the hall and turning up the stairs to my floor. They had guns drawn.

"Here's one of them! Here he is!" Mrs. Morley suddenly screamed, pointing at me.

"All right, put up your hands." The lead guy gave the instructions.

I tried to play it cool. I didn't raise my hands. I acted innocent and puzzled.

"What is all this?" I said. I talked in a loud voice. If Harry hadn't heard the cops storming up the stairs, he'd sure as hell hear me. "Don't point those guns at me. I haven't done anything."

One of the plainclothesmen stepped over to Harry's door and started to fiddle with a key in the lock.

"Come out of there," he called. "Come out with your hands up."

"He's probably a little hung-over," I said. "We had a party last night and he drank too much. Is that why you're here? Did we make too much noise?"

I was really laying the innocent routine on heavy, but it seemed to catch the detectives off guard. They were still waving the guns at me, but I could tell there was a tiny speck of doubt in the corners of their minds. Just enough, at any rate, for them to fall for my next suggestion.

"Look, I'll go in there and get the guy out," I said. "He's probably still drunk. He doesn't realize that you guys are policemen. I'll get him."

There was a short pause.

"All right," the chief cop said. "Go in and bring him out, but remember we're leveling these guns on you every minute."

I opened Harry's door, jumped back, and flattened against the wall in the hallway. Harry let fly with his machine gun. I knew he would. He sprayed the hall but didn't hit any of the cops. One burst of bullets blasted chunks of wood off the wall, and a flying splinter caught one cop in the head. He screamed. He probably thought he'd been shot.

Harry ran into the hall, still firing. The cops rushed the wounded guy down the stairs. They were too busy running to shoot back. Harry swung the machine gun after them. He was firing like a wild man. The bullets ripped into my room. Dolores screamed. I ran to her. One of the bullets had hit her in the thigh. She was bleeding. Eight months pregnant and now a bullet wound.

I tied the wound quickly with a strip of bed sheet and helped her into her slippers and nightgown. I put on my shoes and pants and an overcoat. And I packed my forty-five.

Harry and Wynona were ready and the four of us started down the stairs, Harry and me in the lead, me with the forty-five, Harry with the machine gun. We could see the detectives from the top of the second-floor landing. They were in the lobby. Two of them were tending to the wounded guy. One was on the telephone. A few others seemed to be holding a conference. They didn't see us, and we slipped down to the first floor and made our way through a back hallway that led to an alley.

Mrs. Morley was in the hall.

"My mother's in one of these rooms," she said. "Please don't hurt her."

The bitch had a lot of nerve asking for a favor after pointing me out to the cops.

We went out the back door and up the alley. We came

to a small nook in a stairwell. It was reasonably sheltered. Harry and I told the girls to hide there and wait. We'd come back for them in the car.

We crossed the street to the garage where we'd parked the car. I looked down the street. The cops were milling around the front of the hotel. None of them turned our way. We started across the street.

"Hey, hey! Here they are! Down here!"

It was the garage attendant. He was calling to the cops. He had a gun in his hand. He ran out of the garage and headed down the street toward the hotel. He fired a couple of shots as he ran. They missed by a country mile.

Harry crouched by the door of the garage to keep off the cops. He let go with a couple of blasts, and the cops weren't in any hurry to challenge the machine gun. I ran inside for the Buick but couldn't find it. I gave up the search. I'd take any car, and luckily I found a new Pontiac sedan with a full tank of gas and keys in the ignition.

I gunned the engine and wheeled out onto the street. As I passed the garage door, Harry jumped in the back. He leaned out the window as we made a turn away from the hotel and fired some shots at the cops. I needed plenty of luck because I didn't know Atlantic City's downtown streets. I turned to the right. I thought a right would lead me to the alley where Dolores and Wynona were waiting. I was wrong. The turn took me to a dead end at the Boardwalk. The cops knew we'd trapped ourselves. They waited for us to turn around.

"We'll run right through," I told Harry. "Get the gun ready."

I wheeled the car in a 360-degree turn and raced it straight at the waiting cops. But partway down the street, I saw an alleyway I hadn't noticed before. I twisted the wheel. We skidded and threw burning rubber all over the place, but we made the turn.

We raced down the alley. It was barely wide enough for the car, but it had two or three exits onto other side streets. A mail truck was blocking one. We took another. We made a couple more turns and, as much by luck as by instinct or skill, we found ourselves back in the alley where we left the girls. We stopped in front of the stairwell.

They were gone.

"Maybe the cops got them," Harry said.

We couldn't see any cops, but we could hear the sounds of cars and running feet.

"They'll get us if we hang around here," Harry said.

I nodded my head and pushed down on the gas pedal. I wasn't thinking about it at that moment, but as things turned out, I'd said my last words to Dolores in the stairwell of that back alley.

Harry and I figured the cops would have roadblocks up, and we'd have to run them. We had no trouble escaping from the district around the hotel. All the zooming up and down back streets and alleys must have confused the cops more than it did us. We made our way to a large boulevard that led to a causeway out of the city. The morning had turned into daylight and, as we moved onto the boulevard, we spotted a car ahead with five men sitting in it.

Cops.

I stepped on the gas, and Harry leaned out the window aiming that big, mean machine gun of his. We caught the cops flatfooted. We'd seen them first, and they didn't make a move. They looked at Harry's gun. Then they looked the other way, as if to pretend they weren't cops. We really embarrassed them, and I thought to myself that those cops wouldn't have the nerve even to report that they'd seen us pass by.

We couldn't stay on a main road. We wheeled off at the first side road and swung onto an interurban train track that ran parallel to a highway. We bumped along the ties for about a thousand yards until we reached a farmer's lane. It led us through a series of dirt roads and into a small thicket. We settled down to wait until dusk. It made more sense to drive by night.

It was a rough wait. We had no shirts or jackets, only pants, underwear, and overcoats, and it was plenty cold. We had nothing to eat, nothing to think about except the cops. It took a long time for night to get there. When the sky finally began to turn dark, we pulled out of the thicket and made our way along the dirt roads to the highway. We turned toward Camden, New Jersey, and kicked the car up to sixty. At a Camden station, where I was positive the attendant recognized us, we filled up on gas. But he looked like a guy who was going to keep his mouth shut. He gave us a road map, and we plotted a route across the Delaware River into Pennsylvania and across to the friendly cities of Ohio.

We had to switch cars. In every state, the cops would be watching for our '34 Pontiac, and as we drove through Pennsylvania, we kept our eyes out for another car to steal. On the highway near Allentown, we came across a 1934 Plymouth with doctor's emblems on the rear bumper. It might have been custom-made for us. Nobody stopped a doctor's car. He could drive anywhere at any time of the night without making a cop suspicious.

The driver was alone in the car, and we drove alongside him.

"State police," Harry shouted out the window. "Pull over. We want to talk to you."

Harry climbed into the doctor's car and followed me until we came to a side road. I parked the Pontiac and left the engine running. The gas would burn down and, when the cops found the car, they'd think we had run out of gas and were still on foot somewhere in the area. Then Harry and I pulled away with the doctor.

He was Dr. Horace Hunsicker, a guy in his middle twenties, and he was heading for the state hospital in Allentown after visiting his parents in Philadelphia. He told us that if he didn't turn up for a few hours, no one would miss him. He was the ideal victim for us, and we treated him with absolute politeness. He, in turn, didn't seem especially nervous, and the bunch of us got on like old buddies.

We wheeled across Pennsylvania. Near Altoona, I could see police cars at the side of the road. I expected a trap, but when the cops noticed the doctor's emblems, they waved us through.

We drove all night and all the next day, and by nightfall we had crossed into Ohio. It was time to drop the doctor off.

"Dr. Horace Hunsicker was the ideal victim for us, and we treated him with absolute politeness. He, in turn, didn't seem especially nervous, and the bunch of us got on like old buddies."
— UPI

"We pushed Dr. Hunsicker into the empty town hall. We put a gag around his mouth, and I stuffed a fifty-dollar bill in his breast pocket. Then Harry and I took off for Toledo in the doctor's car."
— UPI

People back at his hospital might be wondering about him. We wanted to get rid of young Hunsicker, but he didn't seem anxious to lose us. He knew that we were criminals, and that was all. Maybe we fascinated him. His radio had been broken when we took over his car, and we hadn't heard any news all day, but Harry fiddled with the thing and made it work. Lowell Thomas came on. The entire Eastern seaboard, he announced was barricaded against two desperate gunmen who had shot their way out of Atlantic City. Thomas gave our names, descriptions, and backgrounds, and all of a sudden our friendly doctor was anxious to leave us.

We pulled into a town called Wadsworth and pushed Dr. Hunsicker into the town hall, which was empty. He was terrified—sure we were going to shoot him. We dragged him into the basement and tied him up next to the furnace, where he'd be warm until someone found him. We put a gag around his mouth, and I stuffed a fifty-dollar bill in his breast pocket to pay his way home. Then Harry and I took off for Toledo in the doctor's car.

Toledo was our refuge. We had contacts there. We abandoned the doctor's car with an empty gas tank in a town in Michigan called Munroe, in a district where there were a lot of empty summer cottages. We hoped the cops would think we'd run out of gas and had hidden in one of the cottages. The tactic would give us time to hole up somewhere.

Harry and I finally settled down in Edith Barry's Toledo whorehouse. I shacked up with Edith, Harry moved in with one of her girls, and we sat back to read the papers and wait for further developments. There was plenty of news. I read that the FBI had taken Dolores to a hospital in Philadelphia detention quarters. The days went by, and I read about the birth of my son. I read that my parents had traveled from Chicago to take the baby home with them, and that Dolores and Wynona were shipped off to Florida to face charges of harboring two criminals.

I read a lot of strange things—and frightening things. I read that the police had found two machine guns under a bridge near Truckee, California, of all places, and that they figured the guns belonged to Harry and me. The cops were looking for us in California, and I couldn't decide whether the story was a police plant or whether they were really stupid enough to think we'd driven all the way to the Coast. I also read that the feds had arrested Doc Barker and charged him with the Bremer kidnapping and that the federal court in Miami, Florida, had convicted Dolores and sentenced her to a women's prison in Michigan for a long term of years.

I couldn't sit around Edith Barry's whorehouse worrying, and Harry and I began to look for a good score in the Toledo area. It didn't take long to agree to take the payroll from the Youngstown Sheet & Tube plant in Warren, Ohio. But it was next to impossible to dig up the right man to take along.

Our troubles were the first hint I'd had that the underworld was changing. The good holdup men were disappearing. When Freddie Barker and I planned a job in the old days, which were really only a few years back, we always had our pick of cool, daring stickup men. Now the good ones were gone. Freddie was dead. Chuck Fitzgerald was wounded. Doc Barker was in jail. Zeigler was dead. There were hardly any top men left. I felt lonely.

We needed just one more man. Three of us could handle it without any problems. The guy who put us onto the score was named Freddie Hunter, and he was a good man, but he couldn't go along with us because Warren was his hometown. To try to find a third partner Harry and I traveled to Tulsa and then back to Cleveland. But nobody we met had the class we were looking for.

My old pal Burrhead Keady put the grim situation in the right perspective when we called on him in Tulsa.

"All that the young guys coming along these days want

to do," he said, "is stick up drugstores and knock over safes. The way you guys did it when you first started out."

It was the same in Cleveland. We couldn't find a big-league operator. But in Toledo, Freddie Hunter came up with a guy named Pinky Mitchell, who had a good reputation as a safe-cracker. On one robbery, a cop had shot Pinky right through the heart, and Pinky lived to tell the tale. We decided to use him for the Warren job, and we laid all our plans, but on the day of the heist Pinky took some pills to calm his nerves and promptly went to pieces. He could hardly stand up. He was useless, and we postponed the job.

Pinky was no good and, as a matter of fact, nothing seemed to be clicking. Freddie Hunter rented an apartment for himself and me in Cleveland, and all night long on the first night we moved in, guys kept knocking on the door. Each time they'd knock, Freddie would open the door and I'd stand in the dark with my machine gun ready. But the guys weren't cops. All they did was ask for girls, especially Irene. Irene was very popular. Next day, I asked the superintendent about the place. It turned out to be a hookers' hangout. I moved out.

Hunter came up with another nominee for the Warren job. His name was Joe Rich, and his credentials weren't ex- actly the best. He was a narcotics addict and he lived with the madam of a whorehouse in Canton, Ohio. Well, at that point I was willing to take along the madam if she was the only person available. I told Hunter that Joe Rich would do and, as it turned out, he seemed a pretty good guy when I met him. He had plenty of nerve, he promised to keep his narcotics habit under control on the day of the job, and he was satisfied to leave all the planning and directing to us.

So the heist was under way, the first job I'd pulled in a long time, a job that seemed especially strange. Why? Because Freddie Barker wouldn't be with me.

KARPIS MAKES GETAWAY BEFORE SPECTACULAR RAID

Hauptmann Loses Last Chance of Escaping Chair

False Tip Takes Police To Entrance of A. & N.

Acting on an anonymous tip, the entrance police rushed to the Navy hospital last night, but after a half hour of fruitless searching abandoned their hunt.

The tip relayed to Chief of Police Joe Wakelin, warned him that Alvin Karpis was hiding in Little Rock and women in communication with...

HOUSE FOUND
WHEN OFFICER
OFFICERS

CAPTURE IS

Eludes G-Men

ALVIN KARPIS

NEW TAX PLAN IS INADEQUATE SAYS FDR AIDE

HELD INSUFFICIENT TO
MEET ADMINISTRA-
TION NEEDS.

PROGRAM IS ASSAILED

Attacked by Ohio Demo-
crat in House as Enemy
of "Every Small Incor-
porated Business Institu-
tion in Country."

Washington, March 30.

BAILEY PLANS NO FURTHER ACTION TO HALT RACING

TIME ELEMENT MAKES
MOVE IN COURT
HERE UNLIKELY.

RULED OUT IN PULASKI

Chancellor Dodge Holds
tion Is Without Jurisdic-
tion in Matter, but Voices
Opinion That Extension
Is Illegal

CALLS FOR INVESTIGATION

(An Editorial)

A staff writer on a Little Rock newspaper dated Sunday March 30, has been the horse races being held at the Oaklawn course has in an expression of opinion.

FOUR CHILDREN DROWN IN POOL OF FLOODWATER

PLAYING WITHIN 50
FEET OF HOME AT
TIME OF TRAGEDY.

BRITAIN FACES CABINET SPLIT ON NEW PARLEY

MILITARY CONVERSA-
TIONS DISPUTED

MERCURY DROP IS PREDICTED FOR ARKANSAS

DAMAGE TO FRUIT
CROPS FEARED FROM
NEW COLD WAVE

BRUNO IS READY TO "TELL MORE" HIS WIFE SAYS

MAKES STATEMENT AFT-
ER VISIT TO CON-
DEMNED HUSBAND

BRUNO DENIED
CLEMENCY BY
PARDON COURT

FOR HOFFMAN
"NO NEW
REPRIEVE"

OUT OF HOPES

15

"My Last Two Jobs"

WE HAD TO TAKE the payroll for the Youngstown Sheet &
Tube plant as it was being unloaded at the railroad station in
Warren. It was delivered by train, and the post office picked
it up for delivery to two different banks. The idea was to
intercept it while it was being switched from train to truck
or, failing that, to stop the truck later and hold up the driver.

Harry, Joe Rich, and I arrived at the depot in the afternoon, ten minutes before the train was scheduled to arrive.
The platform was fairly empty. There weren't many people
around, and the mail truck was waiting in its usual position.

Harry and Joe got out of the car and ambled over to the
platform. They were carrying pistols under their coats, and
I thought they looked a little conspicuous. One of the station
employees thought so too. He walked out of the Railway

202

Express office and gave Harry and Joe a long eye. He called the mail truck driver over. The guy gave them his own personal examination, and the two of them went into the Express office.

By that time, Harry was beginning to come unhinged. He and Joe walked back to the car.

"Do you realize," he said to me, "that we're going to have to kill a lot of people to take this payroll?"

I told them to climb in the car, and I pulled out of the station parking lot. Harry was clearly upset. I drove a couple of blocks hoping to calm him down. A black cat crossed the road in front of the car.

"That was a black cat," Harry said.

"Forget it," I said. "The cat had white marks all over its chest."

"That cat was black as coal," he said.

"Harry, for the chrissake," I said, "a cat isn't going to make a damn bit of difference. The question is, are we going to get this job done or aren't we?"

What a ridiculous situation, arguing over a goddamn cat! I talked tough to Harry. All we had to do was block the mail truck on the street, take it to a garage we had rented, and shake it down. Joe Rich was agreeable. I had to hand it to Joe—he may have been an addict and an inexperienced crook, but he showed a lot of spunk. After a few minutes, Harry got a grip on himself.

We started off again. I angled through the streets until I located the truck. I pulled a few yards out in front of it. I had studied the truck's regular route and I knew, for instance, that it stopped for a certain railway crossing. My idea was to make it stop on the street shortly after it had started up after the crossing.

The plan worked. I watched in my rearview mirror. The truck came to a stop, started up again, and I pulled our truck across the road into its path. The driver hit his brakes. Harry and Joe jumped out of our car with their forty-fives showing. The driver pulled out his own pistol, but he didn't use it. He threw it out the window and held his hands up in the air. A couple of kids happened to be running down the street just as the pistol hit the ground. One of them snatched it and kept on running. Harry and Joe climbed into the cab of the truck and, with me leading the way in our car and the truck following, we set off for our garage.

We hadn't traveled many blocks when I could hear sirens wailing farther back in the city. That kid must have run all the way to the police station with the driver's gun. I didn't panic and didn't try to speed up. We kept moving and made it to the garage.

The driver didn't need much encouragement to open the back of his truck. I found what I wanted underneath the registered bags. It was a sack full of small hard blocks. I recognized the feel of them. The Federal Reserve Banks always shipped their bills in those compact little lumps.

We tied the driver, tossed him in the back of his truck, and pulled away in our car. We drove to an abandoned barn where we'd arranged to meet Freddie Hunter. We ripped open the sack and rolled the bundles of bills on the barn floor. They made a pretty sight. Twelve thousand of the bills were ones. But the rest came in larger bills and, by the time we'd finished, we added up a grand total of $72,000. We split $60,000 into three shares, $20,000 each for me, Harry and Joe. Freddie Hunter got $5,000 for suggesting the score, and the rest went toward various expenses.

Joe Rich had never seen so much money before—$20,000 all for himself and his whorehouse madam. Maybe it was the excitement, but he decided that he needed a fix right there in the barn. He had no water to boil his morphine, so he drained some out of the car radiator. He made a small fire, heated the water and morphine in a can, poured the solution into a syringe, and stuck the hypodermic needle into

"*J. Edgar Hoover* [shown here with an aide] *himself swore to get me, telling the public that crooked politicians were responsible for the FBI's failure to nail me.*" — UPI

his arm. Ten minutes after his shot, he was telling us how we should go after the Federal Reserve Bank in Cleveland.

A few hours after the job the police arrested two alleged members of the Licavolie mob and announced to the newspapers that the mail truck driver had positively identified them as two of the men who robbed the payroll. I was beginning to think that the jails and prisons of North America were filling up with guys serving time for the jobs that I and the other Karpis-Barker members had actually pulled.

It was spring and Harry and I went back to Oklahoma. There we came close to falling into an FBI trap. It was Harry's fault. In Hominy, he ran into Wynona's sister, who had a telegram from Wynona sent from the jail in St. Paul. The telegram asked for $100 for a lawyer's fees, and somehow I didn't like the sound of the whole deal.

Why, for one thing, did the telegram come from St. Paul? What the hell was Wynona doing up there? She hadn't been sent to prison in Minnesota to serve her time for harboring me and Harry. I told Harry to ignore it.

Harry didn't take my advice. He couldn't believe that an old girlfriend of his would pull a fast one on him. He left the $100 with Wynona's sister and told her to send it off to St. Paul. He said he'd call back in a week to see if she'd heard anything more.

Harry didn't go back. It was a good thing, too. The feds were waiting for him. Wynona had agreed to testify for the government in the Bremer case. And while she was in St. Paul, an FBI agent had come up with the telegram idea. He knew that none of Wynona's relatives were rich enough to produce $100. If the telegram did draw money, it would have to come from Harry.

The FBI wasn't about to let up in its hunt for me and the last remaining guys of the Karpis-Barker bunch. J. Edgar Hoover himself swore to get me. He set up a propaganda machine which included publicity releases even stating that

I had sent him a note threatening his life. This was strictly bullshit. He laid the reputation of the bureau on the line. There was absolutely no doubt, he told the newspapers, that his men would bring me in within a few weeks.

Hoover told the public that crooked politicians were responsible for the FBI's failure to nail me. He blasted shady lawyers, ward heelers, elected officials on the take, and all the people that gangsters like me paid off. He claimed that his men had had me cornered in Atlantic City. Only the intervention of crooked public officials kept them from arresting me. Hoover said that when I was finally caught, he'd make me cough up names, dates, places, and fixes. I'd prove out of my own mouth how closely politicians were linked to me.

Freddie Hunter and I took a long drive through the Eastern states in the summer of 1935, and I kept coming on reminders that I was, as the newspapers pointed out regularly, "Public Enemy Number One." Most of the big names in crime were resting in one of two places—prison or the grave. But I was at large, the biggest crook still free, and I hardly ever had a moment to forget my status or reputation.

One day Freddie and I stopped in a small town in Maine and wandered into a drugstore looking for something to read. I browsed through the magazines and found a pulp called *Startling Detective*. Startling! I'd say it was startling. The magazine carried a picture of a girl on the cover and underneath it the line: "The Crimson Career of Alvin Karpis." I thought the girl looked familiar, and after a couple of minutes I recognized her. It was me. The magazine had faked a photograph of me with a dress, a girl's hat, and a few touches of makeup.

Freddie got a big kick out of it, but I wasn't laughing. I knew that in those days lots of guys found the cops on their trail as a result of a tip from some amateur Sam Spade who studied magazines.

We cut into upper New York State, aiming for friendly

territory in Ohio. Our route took us into Saratoga Springs, New York, on, of all days, the opening of the 1935 racing season. The streets were jammed with cars and pedestrians, but I decided it was safe enough to mingle in the big crowds.

We drove down the main street and stopped for a red light. I was at the wheel, and I glanced out the window while I waited for the green. Two men were standing at the corner talking. One looked hard at me, stopped talking to his friend, and stared. I pulled away.

"That son of a bitch on the sidewalk just made me," I said to Freddie.

"Come on," Freddie said, "you're just getting jumpy."

"I'm telling you he made me," I said. "He recognized me. He knows who I am."

I steered the car out of Saratoga Springs and headed for Ohio. By the time we hit Cleveland, the stories were all over the papers.

ALVIN KARPIS SEEN IN SARATOGA SPRINGS was the way one headline put it. The story was that Sonny Whitney, the wealthy racehorse owner, had been warned that somebody was out to kidnap him and how an informant was sharp enough to note down a description of my car, a four-door Ford sedan, which he saw on the main drag of Saratoga Springs. He saw that the license plates were from Ohio, and as I heard from my Cleveland pal Frank Noonan, Mr. Hoover sent his agents into the state in waves. Hoover thought that at last his department would run me to ground.

Freddie and I got rid of the Ford and pulled out for Hot Springs, Arkansas, in a big hurry. We'd already made contacts earlier in Hot Springs. Grace Goldstein was my girlfriend there and Freddie went around with one of Grace's hookers, a girl named Connie. We had a cottage on Lake Catherine for a while, then another at Lake Hamilton. Everything wasn't exactly idyllic. Just because I wanted to take it easy the FBI didn't let up. In fact, they came awfully close to catching me in Arkansas. I'd been out at the Lake Hamilton cottage with Freddie, and we took it in our heads to check out and look over a job in Ohio. I told Grace and Connie to clean the cottage for us, and I wasn't talking about a light dusting.

I meant that they were to wipe every piece of furniture, every utensil, every damn surface in the place that might carry a fingerprint belonging to Freddie Hunter. Freddie's prints were on file with the police. I didn't leave prints because of that operation, but I didn't want the feds to find a finger smudge either. If they found one without so much as a trace of a print, they might decide it was mine. They had, after all, heard about my operation, even though they did maintain that it wasn't possible to remove a person's prints.

The girls did as I told them. The FBI discovered the cottage a couple of days after we vacated it. They dusted the entire place for fingerprints but found nothing that would lead them to us.

Unfortunately, the feds didn't come away entirely empty-handed. They found a medicine bottle in the cottage incinerator. It was Freddie's. He had gonorrhea and the bottle showed a doctor's name on the prescription label. The FBI grilled the doctor and picked up the phony name Freddie was using. It didn't make me feel comfortable to have the feds breezing into my hideouts so soon after I'd left them.

Despite the heat from the FBI, I was still keen to get started on another job. It wasn't necessarily the need for cash that was driving me into action. It was the desire to be busy. I was aching for an exciting heist.

And I had exactly the right job in mind. I'd been mulling it over for weeks. I was going to take a mail train. I thought of the great bandits of the old West, the James Brothers, the Dalton Boys, and all the rest of them. They knocked over trains, and I was going to pull the same stunt.

The one I had my eye on was a mail train that carried

payrolls from the Federal Reserve Bank in Cleveland to small Ohio towns. It deserved to be taken, because on payroll day it carried cash enough to cover the weekly salaries of workers in all the giant mills of Youngstown and the other industrial centers of Ohio.

The job was guaranteed to be a big extravaganza, just like the bank scores Freddie Barker and I plotted a few years earlier. I wished Freddie had been alive to work on it with me. It took good, experienced men to pull off a train job, and in the end I decided to take along five guys: Freddie Hunter; Harry Campbell, who had married a young girl and settled down in Ohio; a fellow named Brock, whom Burrhead Keady recommended to me; Ben Grayson, an experienced robber in his early fifties, just out of prison after serving a sentence for knocking over a post office in Asbury Park, New Jersey; and old Sam Coker.

All the guys were willing to go along on the caper, but I realized some of them were slightly cynical about the sound of it. Ben Grayson probably expressed their opinions one day when he looked me in the eye and asked me a question.

"Just one thing," Grayson said, "who the hell robs a train in this day and age?"

They were a little less doubting when I explained the details. It was one job that I organized down to the last move. I cased the trains, ran the escape roads, plotted the getaway with as much thoroughness as I'd brought to any job I could remember. It was crucial for me to take care in Ohio, because I was hotter in that state than in any of the others. I kept hearing from my Cleveland buddy Frank Noonan that the feds figured I was somewhere in Ohio and that I was working on a major robbery. Their pressure meant that I couldn't slip up on a single item in planning the job. It also meant that I couldn't lay low in Ohio after the score. I'd have to move away fast, and a car wouldn't carry me away with enough speed. I'd use a plane. I'd fly over the roadblocks and zip all the way to Hot Springs before the FBI could pin me down.

My plan meant rounding up a pilot who could fly me out from a small town airport or field. I found the right pilot in Port Clinton, Ohio. His name was Zetzer, and he wasn't partial to policemen. He and his brother owned a marine machine shop in Clinton, and during Prohibition they ran in booze from Canada. Zetzer was a crackerjack pilot, used to relying on pastures as his airstrips. I bought him a light Stinson aircraft, and he and I set out on a dry run.

We flew all the way to Hot Springs. The trip went like a dream. Zetzer was as good as his reputation. I didn't figure to stick around Hot Springs once Zetzer and I arrived there. It was almost as heated up as Cleveland. I'd pull out of Hot Springs by car, and Grace Goldstein and I would drive to her brother's home near Paris, Texas. Texas seemed like the ideal state. I'd never robbed any of its banks. It would be the last state where the feds might think to look for me.

The escape looked solid, and so did the details of the robbery. On November 7, I set it for Garrettsville, Ohio. I knew that on that particular day a train would stop, carrying not one, but two payrolls. They were destined for the mills in Warren and Youngstown.

Garrettsville had the advantage of its short distance from Port Clinton, but it had the disadvantage of its nearness to a college town named Hiram. The college meant students, kids who kept the station platform and parking lot crowded most hours of the day. I didn't like the notion of operating on a big job in a crowd, but that was the risk.

We ran the roads between Garrettsville and Port Clinton at least a dozen times. I got to know every twist and turn. I could even remember the bumps. The idea was for all of us to make the getaway from the depot in one car, with me at the wheel, and then when we hit Port Clinton, we'd hole up there over night. Next day, Freddie and I would fly off with Zetzer, while the others scattered back to Toledo.

The selection of the car for the Garrettsville-Port Clinton run presented a couple of problems. I wanted a four-door Ford V-8 sedan because it had a fast pickup. You could take off in it like in a plane. But for some reason I couldn't locate a dealer in the area who had a V-8 to sell. Never before had I got so insistent about a car. I must have been excited about the job. I offered one dealer a $100 bonus if he'd come through with a new Ford. The dealer couldn't produce a V-8 though, and I finally settled for a new Plymouth.

Well, the car wouldn't have a long life no matter what make it was. I wanted it disposed of as soon as the job was finished. And I told Zetzer that he'd earn an extra fee if he and his brother got rid of the Plymouth in a specific way that I described. They had to cut the car into pieces with torches, then tow the fragments out on Lake Erie and send them to the bottom. The two Zetzers agreed to take on the job.

I handed out duties to each of the five guys who were involved in the heist. One man was to stand by in Cleveland watching the loading of the money bags onto the train from the Federal Reserve Bank truck. He was to make a careful count of everything that went into the payroll and mail car. If, for some reason, nothing was loaded aboard the train, then we'd call the job off. If the FBI had got wind of the score and had posted a bunch of men on the train, then, again, the job would be canceled. Whatever happened in Cleveland, we would have a man standing by and he would phone out to the rest of us in Garrettsville, and we'd take it from there.

The telephone job was crucial but not dangerous, and I assigned it to Sam Coker.

Somebody would have to take the engineer and fireman on the train when it arrived in Garrettsville. We didn't want them to be free to pull the train away if they spotted us holding up the mail car. It wouldn't be a tough job to control them. After all, they weren't armed. I gave that assignment to the new guy. Ben Grayson. He was older than the rest of us, just out of prison, and maybe he'd be a little over-anxious. The two guys in the engine would be just right for him.

I gave Freddie Hunter the chore of covering the parking lot. He was to guarantee that nobody drove out of the place and nobody left the station platform during the short period while we were lifting the payroll. I didn't want a passenger to slip away and set off an early alarm. The rest of us, Campbell, Brock, and me, would take the train. I had the feature role. I would look after the actual heisting of the money from the payroll car. The other two would keep their ears and eyes alert, all set to blast anyone who might resist us.

For our equipment, we lined up three machine guns, a rifle, and five pistols. We filled up a briefcase with dozens of extra clips and, for good measure, I packed a complete medical kit. We also took along a couple of items I'd rarely used in the past—two sticks of dynamite, some caps, and a fuse. I decided they might come in handy. Suppose, I thought, the rail clerks spotted us and suppose they slammed the mail car door shut. How would we bust in? The answer was clear—we'd blast it open. So we packed the dynamite, and I put a couple of cigars in my pockets. I planned to light one of them just before the heist got under way. If we needed to bring the dynamite into the job, I'd use my cigar to set off the wick.

I thought I hadn't missed a trick in sorting out all the elements of the job. But I had. I forgot to consider all the bad habits of the men in my new gang. And a couple of days before the date of the caper, Sam Coker collapsed with gonorrhea. I couldn't really blame him. He'd been in prison for a few years and, when he had his chance at the girls, he went wild. But he latched onto a dirty whore and he came down with more than gonorrhea. He caught a touch of it, and to get rid of it he injected a mild solution of iodine into his body. It finished him. He was carted off to the hospital, and I lost my spy at the depot in Cleveland. I considered a couple of replacements and rejected them. And in the end, I finally forgot all about that part of the plan. We'd take a chance. We'd go ahead on the assumption that the payrolls were on board the train as scheduled.

Coker's disease wasn't the only upset in the few days just before the job. On the very day we were packing our guns, checking the car, and moving toward Garrettsville for the robbery, I found out from the Cleveland papers that the FBI was flooding Cleveland with agents. They knew that I was on the verge of something big and, according to the papers, the feds were set, ready and armed to head me off. But I wasn't calling off the train caper. Not for J. Edgar Hoover himself.

Ben Grayson turned up on the morning of the job looking like a holdup man from out of the past. He had pasted on a fake mustache, one of those long drooping jobs that the old-time train robbers used to wear. He had also rubbed some rouge on his cheeks and on his chin, and he looked like a complete villain.

"For chrissake, Ben," I said to him, "don't move too close to the people on the platform. You'll scare the hell out of them."

Ben laughed. He was a good guy. But he was completely serious about his makeup. He was convinced that somebody might spot him and identify him as a convicted bank robber. He was wrong of course. No one would recognize him. Ben was just going through the typical worries that anyone who had spent time in prison experienced.

The robbery was timed for two forty-five in the afternoon, and a few minutes earlier we were driving through the streets near the depot. A block away from the station we stopped, and Campbell, Grayson, and Brock climbed out. They went along on foot toward the depot, while Freddie and I drove ahead in the Plymouth.

Freddie was packing a machine gun. I told him that not a single person was to leave either the lot or the station until we pulled away. Freddie tucked his machine gun under his overcoat and, when I stopped the car in the parking lot, he stepped out and strolled nonchalantly around the depot.

I surveyed the tracks and platform from the car. Everything looked clear—except for one thing. There were two repairmen perched up on a telephone pole tending to the lines—and they were wearing earphones. If trouble broke out, they could call for help. I began to think that maybe I'd better sic Freddie on them.

Then one of the repairmen distracted me. He started to laugh. He was really broken up. He nudged the other repair guy, and the second man started to laugh too. I couldn't figure it out. Then I looked in the direction they were pointing. It was Grayson. He had just arrived on the platform and, in his eight-inch mustache, he looked as weird as hell. I couldn't blame the telephone guys for laughing, and while I was still wondering what to do about them and their earphones, I heard the train whistle.

I climbed out of the car. I was wearing a topcoat. I had ripped the pocket out of the coat, and I was carrying a machine gun with a twenty-shot clip on a strap slung over my shoulder inside the coat.

The train stopped at precisely the spot I knew it would. The engine hissed. Smoke swept along the platform. About seventy or seventy-five people milled around the station. And the door to the mail car swung open. Two clerks stood looking out of the car.

I glanced down the tracks. Grayson was climbing into the cab of the engine. Brock was standing in the center of

the platform, just about to pull out his gun. Harry Campbell
was taking care of a flagman on the tracks. Freddie was
standing on guard at the top of the parking lot.

I pulled out my machine gun and leveled it at the two
clerks in the mail car. They stared at me. I thought their
eyes would fall out of their heads. But they didn't throw up
their hands. They did something totally unexpected. They ran
back into the car. I hollered at them. I told them to come
out with their hands up. I didn't hear a peep from them.
They were hiding back there.

Well, all right for them. I took a stick of dynamite from
a pocket. I was about to light it. I heard a car start somewhere behind me, out in the parking lot. I turned around
and saw two sights I didn't like.

One, Freddie was taking off, running after two men who
looked like hoboes.

Two, a man and a woman, both with terrified looks on
their faces, were trying to get away in a car.

I forgot the dynamite and ran into the parking lot. I only
had to move a few yards to reach the starting car, and I
flung open the door on the driver's side. I screamed at the
two of them, the man and the woman, to get the hell out
of the car, and I grabbed the car keys and threw them as
far as I could. Freddie arrived back in the lot, and I gave
him a quick, ripping lecture. "Don't leave the lot," I told him.

I hustled back to the mail car. Nothing had changed. The
two clerks were still hiding in the gloom. I threw a stick of
dynamite, unlit, into the car. It landed with a thump close,
I thought, to the clerk.

"I'm going to heave another stick in there," I called out,
"and it'll be burning. You've got five, and I'm counting now.
One, two . . . "

They were in sight by the time I reached "four." There
had been three men in the back of the car, two white guys
and a big, heavy-set Negro. I hadn't noticed the black guy

until he appeared at that moment, and he was a nervy son of a bitch.

"You can't do this, man," he said to me. "Get off with that gun."

I set the machine gun at a single shot and aimed it just over his head. I pulled the trigger. I expected it to fire. It didn't. The hammer fell down, but the slug didn't go off. I was worried. I looked up at the three guys and discovered that there was no reason for me to worry. The sound of the hammer on the gun had scared the hell out of them. They were convinced, and all of them, including the Negro, threw their hands into the air.

By that time, Grayson had the engineer and fireman under control. He led them down the tracks at the end of his gun, and we lined them up with the mail clerks.

I asked who the chief was, and the more elderly of the two white clerks stepped forward. He and I moved into the back of the mail car.

The mail bags were stacked from the floor to the ceiling. I couldn't tell which bags held the payrolls, and the old clerk stood in front of me with an expression on his face that said I would just have to work the problem out by myself.

I leveled my gun at the old guy.

"Buddy," I said, "you know and I know that there's another train coming down the line in a few minutes. If you don't tell me what I want to know in a hurry, that train is going to run right into this one, and there'll be a lot of dead people. I don't care about that, but you might."

The clerk gave in, and I told him the first thing I wanted was the payroll for Warren. He produced a mail bag with a heavy padlock on it.

"Now I want the payroll for Youngstown," I said.

"It isn't on here," the old guy answered.

"I thought you didn't want any trouble," I said.

Harry Campbell climbed into the mail car.

"Look out, Harry," I said. "I'm going to shoot this guy."

I was mad enough to pull the trigger. The old guy began to beg. He said the Youngstown payment had been shipped out the previous day. He pulled out his ledger and showed me that he had signed for only one payroll shipment that day. He wasn't lying, and I was madder than ever. I picked out four bags of registered mail in the hope that maybe there'd be some cash in a few of the letters, and I pushed the five bags to the edge of the mail car. Freddie was standing on the platform, and he yelled at the clerks to load them into the back of the Plymouth.

"Hey, I'm not going to help you rob the train."

It was the mouthy black guy again.

Freddie kicked him in the ass, and he got to work loading the car.

Even with the two or three delays, the entire episode hadn't taken more than a few minutes, and nobody had made a false move. I had to admit too, that the route between Garrettsville and Port Clinton was as clever as any I'd ever laid out. It was full of weird twists and strange cutbacks, and it was guaranteed to throw any possible tails off the track. And it did.

The bad news came in Port Clinton. We pulled into the place where I planned to spend the night before my flight out with Zetzer, and we ripped open the payroll bag. We dumped the bundles of bills on the floor, and they looked like peanuts to my experienced eyes. They were. We counted them up, and the total came to a lousy $34,000. I'd been expecting six times that amount. I was sore, but I told myself that there'd be plenty of other scores. And, besides, I'd accomplished what I set out to do—I'd held up a train in fine style just like the famous old Western bandits.

Zetzer had the Stinson warmed up and ready to take off early the following morning, and he, Freddie, and I flew off without a worry into a bright sunny day.

Grace was in Hot Springs to meet us, and after I'd made Zetzer a present of the plane plus an extra $500 to get rid of the Plymouth back in Port Clinton, Grace and I took off, in a car, for Texas. Freddie and his girlfriend Connie, the hooker from Grace's place, headed for San Antonio to visit Connie's sister. Freddie figured that he'd be safe enough there. And I liked the sound of dropping in on Grace's brother, Leonard, near Paris, Texas. It was one town that wouldn't have a local FBI office.

It didn't, of course. All it had was a lot of poverty. That stretch of country was a sharecropper's nightmare, and I had the old feeling that I was glad to be a robber. I may have been a hunted man. I may have been wanted in eight or nine states, wanted by the FBI and by the postal authorities. But at least I wasn't dirt poor. And, momentarily, I felt pretty good.

16

"We Kept Shifting Locations... We Had to Present the Feds with Moving Targets"

THROUGH THE LAST months of 1935 and the early winter of 1936 I had to keep moving—to keep some distance between me and the feds. The FBI was really collecting its forces to pin me down.

It seemed to be carrying the search into almost every state in the Union. One news story reported that forty FBI agents surrounded an apartment house in New York City on a tip that I was inside. They dragged a young guy out of the place and threw him into jail. It turned out his only crime was the ownership of a car with Oklahoma license plates. The feds thought it was my car.

In Cleveland and Toledo they were ransacking all my old haunts and they were keeping a constant watch on the apartment in Chicago where my parents and my baby son lived.

They thought there was an outside chance I'd risk a visit to the baby I'd never laid eyes on. But I couldn't.

Another news story came along that reported sixty FBI agents converging in Little Rock, Arkansas. Hoover said that his men were merely holding a regional conference, but the underworld news told me differently. The feds were in Little Rock following up a lead they had that I was holed up somewhere in the area. They were almost right—I was living in Hot Springs at the time.

Two or three weeks after the train job and the short cooling-off trip through Texas, Freddie and I moved back to Hot Springs. We didn't settle in any one house. We kept shifting locations. It wasn't good for our nerves to spend too much time in the same few rooms. We had to present the feds with moving targets.

In early December, we stayed for a while in a house right at an intersection. There was a stop sign under the window in Freddie's bedroom and, at some point every night, there would be a sudden squeal of brakes from the street. Freddie couldn't get used to the sound. Every time there was a squeal, he'd spring up, grab his gun, and run to the window.

"What do you think you'll find out there?" I asked him one night.

"The cops," he said.

We moved out of that house the next day.

Grace rented us a cottage on a mountainside on the outskirts of Hot Springs. It was isolated and suited me perfectly. But a couple of weeks after we set up in the place, Freddie brought two visitors around, Sam Coker and Burrhead Keady. I didn't like it. I didn't want anybody to know where I was staying. I especially didn't want Burrhead to know anything about me. Burrhead was a nice guy, but he was a lush, and guys who drank usually talked.

We moved again.

Grace found us another house. It was on Malvern Road,

which ran between Hot Springs and Malvern, Arkansas. The house, built on a hill that overlooked Lake Catherine, was lovely. It belonged to a wealthy real estate operator named Woodcock, and it came with a couple of safety features I liked—bright outside lights and two barking dogs.

When I wasn't worrying about the FBI, I was worrying about the postal authorities. They'd been hot after me ever since the payroll train caper, and they were handling the search with better results than the feds.

They had scored a big victory up in Tulsa. There'd been a bad shoot-out there that had riled up the Tulsa police, and they conducted a series of raids on all the joints around the city. In one of them, they busted into a safe that Burrhead Keady owned, and some of the money in the safe came from the train job. One of the guys on the job, Brock, had turned the money over to Burrhead to change into clean bills for him.

The postal people got in on the act, and it didn't take them long to trace the money back to Ohio. They grilled Burrhead, and he told them about Brock and the train robbery. They got their hands on Brock, and he really sang. He confessed to them about Edith Barry's whorehouse in Toledo, about how it was a traditional hideout, and all the details of the train heist, including the part about my plane trip from Port Clinton to Hot Springs.

That piece of information brought the postal cops and the FBI into Arkansas in greater numbers than ever before. A friendly guy who worked at the airport told us that some postal cops had been showing my picture and Freddie's around. Brock's statements must have led them to the airport, and they found someone to identify Freddie, but nobody owned up to knowing or recognizing me. I gave the airport guy $500 for the tips.

Somehow the postal people got on to Freddie's girl, Connie. They hired a fellow to take her out on the town with instructions to fill her full of booze and let her talk. Connie was too smart. She poured the liquor under the table, and it was the undercover man who drank too much. He told her who he was and what he was up to. Then he suggested that the two of them turn Freddie in, collect a reward, and run off together. She brushed him off and reported the whole episode back to Freddie and me.

We didn't know how much reward money the government and the different states were offering for us. We heard that Hoover guaranteed $5,000 to anyone who produced information that led to our arrest.

Grace was the next person to report some funny business.

"The FBI paid a guy I know a thousand dollars to take me out," she said. "He's an undertaker."

"An undertaker?"

I was understandably surprised. Who the hell would want to go out with a mortician? I had to laugh.

"They think I know where you are and I'll tell this guy," she explained.

Things didn't look good, and sometimes I thought I should buy a place hundreds of miles away, in some isolated place where I had no past connections. Maybe in Oregon somewhere, or in Washington State. The feds would never consider looking for me in places like that. But, for the moment, Oregon and Washington had to remain dreams. I still had some scores I wanted to see through.

I made a date with Grace to meet her in two weeks' time on a side road that ran into the Hot Springs-Arkadelphia highway, and Freddie and Connie and I set out for Texas in our cars. I went first to Grace's brother's place and left a suitcase with him for safe keeping. My machine guns were in it. Then I met Freddie and Connie at a tourist camp in Rockport, Texas. It was early April, the weather was warm and peaceful, and we intended to settle in for a little relaxation and fishing.

Then I made the mistake of picking up a newspaper. The

FBI had raided our house in Hot Springs. The story was short on facts and long on speculation. It said that some men had been picked up in the house, according to rumors, and that the rumors indicated the men probably included Freddie and me. They were wrong, but Freddie and I decided that if someone had been arrested in the house and if the someone confessed that we were in Texas, then Texas wasn't a safe place. We packed up and headed on.

We drove to New Orleans and hung around a few days. As the time for my meeting with Grace grew closer, we drove to Arkadelphia and rented two cottages, one for Freddie and Connie, the other for Grace and me.

Grace kept the appointment on the side road, and she looked as if she'd been through hell. She was pale and exhausted and said that a few days after Freddie and I left Hot Springs, the FBI raided her place in the Hatterie Hotel. Early one morning, six or seven agents piled into her room, some from the FBI, some from the postal department, and they started grilling her. They wanted to know where I was and they threatened her with jail, beatings, and all kinds of trouble. She kept her mouth shut, claimed she didn't know me, and eventually the cops went away.

Then Grace made a mistake. She went up to the house on Malvern Road one night to pick up something I'd left there. She turned on a light. She shouldn't have touched a switch. I'd warned her not to. The FBI, as I suspected, had found the place and were watching it. They saw the lights and figured I was in there. They let Grace leave, and then they hit the house.

They really did a job, according to Grace. They rained bullets in the windows. They blew out the door. They lobbed in some flares. One flare landed on a bed and set a fire. When it kept on burning, a few agents went in to put out the blaze. That was when they discovered that the house was empty.

The wreckage of the house got J. Edgar Hoover into hot

water. A U.S. Senator named Joe Robinson happened to be a close friend of Woodcock, the guy who owned the Malvern Road place, and the Senator blasted Hoover on the floor of the Senate for the FBI's failure to be certain someone was in the house before they launched their assault. The rumor was that Hoover himself had led the Hot Springs attack, but nobody confirmed the truth of the story. It was a bad time for Hoover all around for a couple of weeks. He also took a public pounding for hiring a press agent, a guy named Courtney Riley Cooper, who was paid a fabulous salary to shine up Hoover's image. Some Senators wanted to know something about Hoover's other expenses—for instance, the amount he had spent on stool pigeons to try to track me down.

I enjoyed reading about Hoover's difficulties, but I had worse problems of my own. At my meeting with Grace, I told her to drive to her brother's place and pick up my guns. Then she was to wait a couple of weeks and join Freddie, Connie, and me at our apartments in New Orleans. The three of us went back to Louisiana. But Grace joined us with bad news. The feds had called on her brother and were still watching his house. They hadn't found the guns. When her brother read about the raid in Hot Springs, he'd immediately taken them out into his fields and buried them. They were protected from the FBI, but there was no way that I could get them.

Grace and I decided to take a holiday, and we hit the road. We drove a new Terraplane coupe, and we stopped first in Sarasota, Florida, where we fished and visited the Ringling Brothers Circus Museum. We carried on like tourists, drifting north to Tampa and Pensacola, then across to Biloxi and Gulfport in Mississippi.

The trip wasn't completely blissful, though. I kept hearing radio bulletins that jerked me back to reality. I heard that the district attorney in St. Paul had finally received enough FBI evidence to indict me for the Hamm kidnapping from way

back in June, 1933. The feds had also charged old Chuck
Fitzgerald for the same caper. They arrested him out in
Beverly Hills, where he was living in a swank apartment
building. I was glad to hear that Fitzgerald had apparently
put together some money for himself.

I was also happy to hear about the judge who had sentenced Dolores to her jail term for harboring me. This guy
had been very rough on Dolores, barring the press and public
from the trial, allowing Dolores to plead guilty without being
represented by a lawyer, and then handing her three concur-
rent five-year sentences. But he finally got his own licking.
The papers I read told how he was impeached on a fee-split-
ting charge that involved his former law partner and was removed from the bench.

Back in New Orleans, Freddie wanted to plan a little business with me, and I took Grace home to Hot Springs. Freddie
liked the thought of taking a small bank near where he was
staying in New Orleans. I had a couple of other ideas. In
Mississippi I'd seen a big construction project going up called
Pickwick Dam that must have had a good-sized payroll. I took
a look at another possibility, a train score in Iuka, Mississippi.

On my way back to New Orleans I drove through Memphis
and Jackson, and I found my picture on the front pages of all
the newspapers. Every city had picked that day to run stories
and pictures of big criminals still at large. I recognized an
old FBI tactic at work. They made a practice of flooding certain regions with crime stories in the hope that the guys they
were after would hole up someplace. Then, if the feds were
lucky, the hideout would be a place they had already staked
out.

I drove to my apartment on St. Charles Boulevard. Afterward, I went over to Freddie's apartment on Jefferson Parkway. He and Connie were still there.

There was something in the air, but I couldn't explain what
it was. Freddie came out with a couple of incidents that in-

creased my anxiety. He said that a couple of days earlier his landlady had suddenly called at the apartment. She kept some of her furniture in one of Freddie's spare rooms, and she said she wanted to show it to a buyer. Freddie agreed, and the landlady brought in a sharp-looking character in his late thirties or early forties.

"Now that I think of the guy," Freddie told me, "he didn't seem like the type who'd be interested in a bunch of second-hand furniture."

Only the day before, Freddie went on, he'd noticed four guys carrying suitcases up to an apartment on the floor above his. He'd asked the janitor about them and had been told that they were Harvester salesmen who were keeping the apartment for some girls. The story made sense, but I didn't like it. The furniture buyer and the Harvester men could easily have been feds.

I asked Freddie to come out with me for a drive. I wanted to take my car to a garage for servicing. But first, I had some guns in the trunk that I wanted to switch to Freddie's car. We drove out to Lake Pontchartrain and turned into a deserted street where we transferred the guns. I kept my forty-five with me and we drove back to New Orleans to the United Motors Garage.

I left my car, and Freddie and I took a slow, casual drive around the city.

"I'm not sure about this," Freddie said after a few minutes, "but I think somebody's tailing us. The car's got two guys in it. It's a coupe, a maroon-colored job."

I had seen a coupe at Lake Pontchartrain, and it seemed to me now that it had been maroon.

"Just circle around and see what happens," I said. "Keep making right turns until you've gone all around the block. See if they follow."

We made the turns. Freddie kept looking in his rearview mirror. He couldn't see the coupe. If it had really been following us, it had stopped. We drove home to Freddie's apartment.

It was the middle of the afternoon, and Connie asked us if we'd go out and pick up some strawberries for supper. We said we would, but neither of us was especially excited about the idea of going back into the streets.

I told Freddie to start the car. I'd watch from the window with my gun. If he saw anything suspicious, he was to feel around in his pockets, pretend he'd forgotten something, and come back into the apartment. He strolled outside, took a casual look around, and climbed into the car. Everything was clear. I followed him outside. I stood on the sidewalk and looked up at the apartment that the four guys had rented. They could have cut me down at that moment from their window. I felt a definite chill.

Freddie and I drove to the grocery store. He parked and went in for the strawberries. I waited in the car. A DeSoto pulled up beside me. A stocky guy in a Panama hat was behind the wheel. He looked at me and stared for a moment. Freddie came back and I told him about the DeSoto and the stocky guy. He'd seen them, he said, a couple of days earlier. I told him that we were just overreacting.

We took the strawberries back to Connie. The temperature was in the high eighties, and she had changed into white shorts and a halter.

We sat around for a while, but I couldn't keep still. I walked to the drugstore down the street. I bought a pack of Chesterfields and a copy of the *Reader's Digest*. I noticed a guy on a bench wearing a suit and a felt hat. Strange clothes for such a hot day. I walked back to the apartment.

I told the garage that I'd be back for my car at five o'clock, and at four fifty I asked Freddie to drive down with me. I didn't want to wear my jacket in all that heat. I left it hung over a chair. Without the jacket, I couldn't carry my forty-five. There'd be no place to conceal it, so I took it out of my

"The postal people got on to Freddie Hunter's girl, Connie, and hired a fellow to take her out on the town, fill her full of booze and let her talk. Connie poured the liquor under the table and the undercover man drank too much." — UPI

belt and slipped it under the cushion of the sofa. I put on my straw hat, and Freddie and I walked out to the sidewalk.

The car was parked on Jefferson Parkway. I looked down the street. The man in the suit and felt hat was still sitting on the bench. I also noticed two guys on the sidewalk. They were beefy tough-looking men in suits, both in their fifties. They didn't look like FBI men, and Freddie and I walked past them to the car.

I told Freddie that I'd drive. I unlocked the door and slid behind the wheel. Freddie walked around to the other side and, after I opened his door from the inside, he climbed into the seat beside me. I wheeled down my window to get some air. Then I put the key in the ignition and turned it. I started to push the starter with my foot and, at that exact moment, a car cut sharply in front of our car and stopped at the curb. Five men climbed out very quickly.

For one brief, silly moment, I thought they were from a car pool and were just getting back from their offices.

Then I heard a voice at my window.

"All right, Karpis," the voice said, "just keep your hands on that steering wheel."

I turned my head slightly to the left and my temple bumped into the barrel of a gun. It was a 351 automatic rifle. I caught a quick glimpse of the guy holding the gun, and the thought flashed through my head that he fitted Freddie's description of the guy who'd come to look at the furniture.

I held my head steady, looking straight out the window. I had no choice. Two men were leaning over the hood of the car that had cut in front of us. Each of them was aiming a machine gun at my head. Three other men were crouched in the street. They had pistols, drawn and ready. None of these guys had yet bothered to identify themselves. But then I didn't need hints. The whole operation had FBI written all over it.

Out of the corner of my right eye, I could see Freddie

sliding quietly out his door. Nobody paid any attention. He made it to the sidewalk and disappeared from my sight.

The guy with the rifle was getting more excited about me by the second.

"Okay, Karpis," he said, "get out of the car and be damn careful where you put your hands."

I slid out of the seat, keeping my hands in plain sight. I stood up on the street and, as I did, I heard voices call out from above me. I looked up and saw three or four guys lean-

"It was bedlam. More and more agents materialized. 'Keep those hands in the air,' one agent said. 'Put them down at your sides,' another called."

THE GIANTS

THE GIANTS

ing out of the windows of the apartment above Freddie's. They were calling to the other agents.

"Stop that man on the sidewalk," one of them was hollering. "Stop him. He's getting away."

He was talking about Freddie, who had made it about one hundred feet down the street. He was walking casually as if he had nothing to do with the whole messy business. But he hadn't walked far enough. He was caught. One of the guys with the machine guns sprinted after him and led him back to the group around the car.

It was bedlam. More and more agents materialized. The only guy I didn't notice was the man in the felt hat and the suit who'd been sitting on the bench near the drugstore. I guess he wasn't an agent. He wasn't missed. There were enough people around, many of them calling out orders that contradicted instructions somebody else had called out a second earlier.

"Keep those hands in the air," one agent said.

"Put them down by your sides," another standing beside him called.

"Stand right where you are. Don't move, now, don't move."

"Sit down on the running board. Hurry up. Move."

I turned slightly and I was facing a man holding a Thompson machine gun. He was wearing a Palm Beach suit and a Panama hat, and he looked cool and collected. He seemed to be in charge. The gun was steady in his hand, which was more than I could say for the guy standing behind me with the rifle. He kept jabbing me in the back. I couldn't see him, but I had the impression that his hands were trembling.

The man with the machine gun spoke to me in a calm and assured voice.

"Karpis, do you have a gun with you?"

"No."

I was wearing a shirt, pants, and a hat. I didn't know where I'd be hiding a gun.

"All right, Karpis," he said, "I'm putting the safety on this gun. There's no need for anybody to get hurt here."

He snapped the safety, and I asked him about the guy behind me with the rifle. "Please, tell that guy to put his safety on," I said. "He's liable to kill me." The guy with the rifle heard what I said and he was madder than hell.

"Wait till we get you downtown, Karpis," he said. "I'll show you who's running things."

By that time, the action had attracted a huge crowd. There were a couple of dozen FBI agents and at least a hundred spectators. The commotion was terrific. But I could see that some of the men with the guns had turned their attention to another chore. They were looking over toward the corner of the building and they were waving their arms.

I heard one guy shouting, "We've got him. We've got him. It's all clear, Chief."

A couple of others shouted the same thing. I turned my head in the direction they were looking. Two men came out from behind the apartment. They'd apparently been waiting in the shelter of the building, out of sight, while the guys with the guns had been leveling at Freddie and me. They began to walk across the lawn and sidewalk toward the crowd. One was slight and blond. The other was heavy-set, with a dark complexion. Both were wearing suits and blue shirts and neat ties. They walked closer, and I recognized the dark, heavy man. I'd seen pictures of him. Anyone would have known him. He was J. Edgar Hoover.

I knew at that moment, for sure, that the FBI had finally nailed me.

17

"Put the Cuffs on Karpis"

J. EDGAR HOOVER'S ARRIVAL at the scene on the street in New Orleans didn't mean that everything fell into order. The chaos continued. There were so many agents, so many guns, and so many spectators that no one could seem to control the mess. Freddie and I stood in the middle of the mob scene. It was as if one army had captured another—with one exception: The captive army numbered only two guys.

"Handcuff him," someone called out. "Put the cuffs on Karpis."

Nobody in the crowd of agents had brought handcuffs. The cool guy with the machine gun took off his tie and handed it to another agent, who wrapped it around my wrists. Someone else came forward with a set of leg shackles and started to fasten them around my ankles. He locked the shackle

235

on my left leg, but he couldn't make the right shackle fit. He fumbled and fiddled until finally someone told him to forget it.

"We can't stand around here all day," someone else said. "Look at the crowd. There must be five hundred people in the street."

In all the confusion, Hoover didn't say anything that I heard. He was just one of the agents milling around, trying to decide what to do with us.

Finally, after a few more minutes of shoving and shouting, a car pulled over to the curb, and a swarm of agents began to jostle me into the front seat. The fed at the wheel was a guy named Clarence Hurt from Oklahoma City. Another agent moved in from the passenger side, and I sat in the middle, my hands bound with a tie and my left leg trailing an iron shackle. I still had my straw hat on.

I looked over my shoulder into the back seat. There was Hoover. He sat at one window. His number one right-hand man, Clyde Tolson, sat at the other. And Connie was between them. I hadn't noticed her in all the earlier commotion, and she looked plenty scared. Both of us had lost track of Freddie.

Hurt pulled the car away from the crowd and started down Jefferson Parkway. And immediately it became clear that he was lost.

"Does anybody know where the post office building is?" he asked.

"I can tell you," I said.

"How do you know where it is?" Tolson asked.

"Well," I answered, "we were thinking of robbing it."

Nobody laughed. I was actually only kidding. I hadn't even considered robbing the post office. Besides, Hurt didn't want to drive to it. He was confused. The FBI offices were in the Federal Building, not the post office.

I was hustled into a room and plunked down at a desk

facing Hoover. For the first time, he had something to say to me.

"Well, Karpis," he began, "is it a relief to have it all over with?"

I told him that I was glad the tension was over with but that I wasn't very happy about getting caught.

"You're lucky you're still alive," he said. "Do you realize that?"

I shrugged.

"Did you have any machine guns in your car or in your apartment?" he asked.

"No."

"But you do own some machine guns?"

"Yeah," I answered, "but I left them with some friends."

"Some friends? What friends?"

"Some friends in Cleveland."

"For the first time Hoover had something to say to me. 'Now, Alvin,' he said in a smooth tone, 'suppose you give us the names of some of your friends in Cleveland.' " — UPI

"Cleveland? Well, now."

Hoover smiled and looked at the other agents grouped at the desk, as if to say that this was how you handled an interrogation.

"Now, Alvin," he said in a smooth tone, "suppose you give us the names of some of your friends in Cleveland."

I told him that he could save all of us a lot of wear and tear if he'd try a different line of questions. I told him that I wasn't going to give out the names of guys I'd worked with who were still free and out of jail. I said that I wouldn't talk names even if they started smacking me around.

"We're not going to do anything like that to you, Alvin," Hoover said, sounding slightly hurt that our nice communication had broken down. "We're not going to hurt you in any way."

Another agent took that moment to butt into the conversation.

"Karpis," he said, "let's have a look at that diamond ring of yours."

"What diamond?" I said.

I was wearing a diamond ring, but I'd turned it on my finger and the stone was facing on the palm side of my hand. I didn't want the agents looking at the ring if I could help it. The stone was worth $4,000, and it had been a gift to me from some fellows in Cleveland in appreciation of services rendered.

"We know all about the ring," another agent piped up. "We know how much it's worth and where it came from. Let's have a look. We're not going to take it away from you."

I showed it to them. They oohed and ahed. It was a strange scene—a bunch of FBI agents admiring a diamond on the hand of Public Enemy Number One.

"Boy, I'd sure love a ring like that," one agent said to me.

"You could have had it," I said. "All you had to do was warn me in advance about my arrest."

The jokes over the ring ended the funny business. For the next couple of hours Hoover retired from the room, and other agents took turns asking me questions about a whole bunch of subjects. The room, during the period, was mobbed with FBI men, some on phones, some holding conferences, some quizzing me. And I noticed that at one point Freddie Hunter was leaning against a wall off to the side. The agents totally ignored him.

The grilling wasn't especially enlightening, though I managed to pick up a couple of interesting facts. One agent told me how lucky Freddie and I really had been. He said that the FBI had been anticipating a shoot-out and that all the agents were preparing to go into the apartment firing when we happened to wander out to the car. We took them by surprise, and the surprise accounted for a lot of the confusion in the street. The agent also told me that the two guys in front of the apartment when we came out, the two who didn't look like agents, really weren't regular run-of-the-mill agents. They were two former Texas Rangers, real tough guys, the kind the FBI always called in when they expected a big shoot-out.

While we were still sitting in the room, I said I wanted to call a lawyer. It made sense that I should have access to a lawyer. After all, I was under indictment in the Hamm kidnapping and, it turned out, in the Bremer kidnapping as well. I thought I should have been taken before a United States commissioner or a federal judge. I should have had bail set. I should have had a lawyer. The agents in the room refused to listen to my requests. Instead they brought me a paper to sign. It was a waiver, a document that would allow them to forget all legal proceedings in New Orleans and take me straight to St. Paul to face the kidnapping charges. I said okay, I'd sign as long as they'd give me a lawyer in St. Paul. They agreed and I signed.

At eight o'clock that night, May 1, three hours after my

arrest, Hoover and some of his agents took me on board a
brand-new Douglas aircraft that the FBI had chartered from
Trans World Airlines. We flew all the way to St. Paul in
the dark, and it was a rough flight. The weather was poor,
and the agents told me a few things that weren't calculated
to comfort me.

"We arrested your St. Paul pal, Harry Sawyer, down in
Mississippi," one agent said to me, "and we shook him up.
We told him that if he didn't talk we'd take him up in a
plane just like this one and throw him out the window."

"Is that what you're going to do with me?" I asked.

"Think it over."

An agent named Connelly started to ask me about some
past jobs.

"Maybe we can give you a break if you go along with us,"
he said. "We know about your caper in Chicago in 1933,

*"We flew all the way to St. Paul in the dark, and it was a rough
flight. The weather was poor, and the agents told me a few things
that weren't calculated to comfort me."* — St. Paul Dispatch

the one where you guys killed the policeman. We could have you electrocuted for that one."

I didn't answer.

"We know everything about it," Connelly went on. "We even know that it was Bolton who shot the diamond out of Doc Barker's ring, and we know Bolton shot the cop. Everybody on that job could get the chair."

I spoke up.

"Okay, if that's all true," I said, "why not just hand me and Bolton and all the others over to the people in Chicago? We don't have to go through all this stuff on the kidnapping charges."

Connelly backed down a little way.

"I don't think we'll do that," he said. "If we tried Bolton in Chicago and he was convicted as a cop killer, then he wouldn't have much use as a government witness against you and the others in the Hamm trial. Nobody believes a cop killer. And we're not taking any chances on not getting a conviction in the Hamm case. That's the one we care about."

At least I'd learned something during the flight up to St. Paul. They were concentrating on Hamm, and I understood why. The FBI looked pretty stupid when they charged the Touhy Gang with the job and they looked even more stupid when the courts didn't convict the Touhys. The feds were out to clean up their records, and I was the boy who could do it for them. They had to convict me in the Hamm kidnapping.

The plane landed at the St. Paul airport early in the morning. It was Saturday, May 2, and by nine o'clock, the feds had me locked up in the FBI offices in the Federal Building downtown. They put handcuffs on me—real cuffs, not a necktie—and they chained shackles around my ankles and locked the other ends of the shackles to a steam radiator. I felt like an animal.

Hoover came in, and I asked about a lawyer. I said that

the agents in New Orleans had promised me a lawyer in St. Paul.

Hoover looked mad. He had lost the suave, friendly tone he had used down South.

"You've got a lot of nerve," he said to me. "Do you really think you're going to get a lawyer after all you've put us through?"

"That's why I signed the waiver," I said. "I was promised a lawyer up here."

Hoover called me a son of a bitch, and then he turned to the agents who were in the room.

"I want a signed confession from this man for every crime he ever committed in his life," Hoover thundered. "I want to know the names of all the people who were in on his crimes. I want all the details, and I don't give a damn how you get them. If he starts to lie, kick his teeth in for him."

He told them to question me in relays, not to let me sleep, and not to give up until I'd told them everything I knew and agreed to tell it all over again in front of a grand jury.

Then Hoover turned back to me.

"Okay, Karpis, I'm going to Washington," he said. "But I'll be getting reports on you every few hours, and if you don't cooperate, I'll make it my business to see that you're electrocuted."

He paused a second and seemed to soften a little.

"If you go along with us," he said, "I might decide to give you a break."

Then Hoover and a couple of his senior officers walked to the door, opened it, and stepped out. No one in the room spoke. It was so quiet in there I could hear the sound of the agents' breathing. One agent went over to the door and opened it a crack.

"Has he gone?" another agent asked.

The guy at the door nodded, and everyone let out long sighs.

None of the agents spoke to me for almost an hour. I spent the time just looking around the room. It was an ordinary police room, with a couple of filing cabinets, a desk, a dictaphone, and a door into a vault where they probably stored their guns. There was a window above the radiator that I was chained to, and through the crack between the bottom of the blind and the bottom of the window, I could see out into downtown St. Paul. I could spot the Lowry Hotel, a place where I'd often stayed in the days when I was free.

Eventually an agent came over and snapped my attention back to the fix I was in. The agent was a sawed-off little character with jug ears. His name was Sam McKee and he talked tough.

"We're going to lay down some ground rules," he said. "We call the shots. We ask the questions. You give the answers. If you don't, you're in trouble. It's that simple."

And McKee's warning was the beginning of the grilling. I didn't realize it at the moment, but I was to be shackled to the radiator for most of the next four and a half days. I was to be questioned almost without letup. I was to be fed only intermittently, and I was to be allowed out to the bathroom only at night when no outsiders, no one from the press or public, would be around to take a look at my condition.

Much of those days went by in a blur. I got punchy on fatigue. Occasionally I'd doze off, but only for a second. The agents made sure I didn't stay out too long—they'd punch me awake. I asked for cigarettes from time to time. The agents laughed. They laughed even harder when I asked for a lawyer.

The agents seemed to be coming in for a shot at me from all over the country. I heard a dozen different accents. Many of them treated the occasion as kind of a convention, an opportunity for getting together with their old buddies in the bureau. They'd quiz me and then retire for a little conversation with their pals. At one point, I heard two agents bragging to each other about how they'd tracked down the guys who robbed the bank at Redwood Falls, Minnesota. They went into great detail about the brains and guts it had taken to catch the robbers and, as I listened to them, I began to wonder what they were talking about. The bank in Redwood Falls had only been robbed once, back in 1932, and the men who pulled the job had never been caught. I knew—my gang handled the score.

That was one of the few small moments of satisfaction I enjoyed. The rest of the hours and days were taken up with endless questioning. The things the agents wanted to know covered a fantastic range of subjects. They asked me about the police chiefs of several towns. Did I know them? Had I made any deals with them? Were they crooked? They wanted to know about the mayor of Hot Springs and about the gambling syndicate in Cleveland. And what about St. Paul? What about Jack Peifer and his connections with the police department?

"Who was the fix in Miami?" one agent asked.

"Who helped you get away when we were looking for you in Cuba?" another demanded.

"Tell us about the money-changing boys in Reno."

"What do you know about the setup at city hall in Toledo?"

The questions never seemed to stop. They covered every kind of crime and almost every state in the country. Some of the questions I couldn't answer even if I'd been inclined to. I just didn't know what the agents were talking about. But I did know the answers to many others. And when I did, I kept my mouth shut. I wasn't going to tell those FBI guys anything. Let them find out some other way, I kept saying to myself.

They tried all kinds of ploys to squeeze the answers out of me. McKee, the short, tough agent, handed me a stack

KARPIS HELPERS SOUGHT IN NEW DRIVE BY G-MEN

Startling Arrests Hinted; Mobster Grilled Day and Night by Sleuths in Shifts.

HAMM RANSOM PASSERS ONE OBJECT OF SEARCH

Alvin Karpis, branded a "yellow rat" by J. Edgar Hoover, who led his G-men in the capture of the gunman-kidnaper, was undergoing intense questioning early today, that Federal agents...

Addis Ababa in F[...] Peril Thousands

STEP RIGHT IN, MR. KARPIS!

[D]ERADO CRESTFALLEN FEDS SURROUND PLANE WITH MACHINE GUNS, RIFLES

[Re]d Kidnaper of Hamm and Bremer Is Bound Hand and Foot With 15 Pounds of Manacles on 1,530-Mile [Ove]rnight Trip From New Orleans; Red-Haired Girl [and] Fred Hunter Are Left Behind.

[HOO]VER, CHIEF INVESTIGATOR, HEADS [G]ROUP WHICH ESCORTS OUTLAW TO CITY

[Wi]lted and bewildered, Alvin Karpis, 26-year-old [Publi]c Enemy No. 1, was brought to St. Paul by airplane [at 7:]47 A. M., today to face charges of kidnaping Edward [Bremer] and William Hamm for $300,000 ransom.
[...] Federal Bureau of In-

Search for Two Mobsters Begins As Agents Finish Grilling of Karpis

[Hun]t Spread After Stassen [C]onfers With G-Men; Kid[n]aper's Bail Increased to [H]alf Million Dollars.

['HARD]LY', HE SAYS OF [Q]UERY ON RAISING IT

[Al]vin Karpis, sullen and defiant, [fac]ed temporarily an inquisition [at th]e hands of Department of Jus[tice] agents shortly after 4 P. M. [Wedne]sday as those agents and their [associa]tes over the United States [bega]n an intensive hunt for two [more] mobsters whose identity has [not] been disclosed.

[Kar]pis, who replied, "Well, hard[ly,"] when asked if he could pro[vide a] half million dollars bail for [his re]lease, was taken to the Ram[sey c]ounty jail to await arraign[ment a]nd possible trial for kidnap[ing of] William Hamm Jr. and Ed[ward] G. Bremer.

[Addi]tion of $100,000 bail to the [$400,0]00 already demanded resulted [from a] duplication of indictments [in all] orders in the Bremer kid[nap]case. Two indictments, one [chargi]ng him with the Bremer ab[duction] and one with conspiracy [to do the] crime were returned by a [local] grand jury here some time [ago. A] part of the Karpis-Barker [gang ha]d previously been indicted [for cons]piracy in the kidnaping.

[OTHE]R CHARGES STAND.

[An e]arlier kidnaping indictment [stands] as a charge on which to try [Karpis an]d the gang and was not nolled [when] Karpis when later two true [bills] were returned against him. [...] was met in the Depart-

a "mystery" [...] were left in New Orleans, [whe]re Karpis once prospered in [his] youthful outlawy. He was [cow]ed when he stepped from the [...] had none of the defiance of his [...] "would never be taken alive."

BIG RECEPTION COMMITTEE.

A reception committee of 30 [f]ederal agents, armed with ma[c]hine guns and rifles, and a con[ting]ent of newspaper reporters [and] photographers, arrived at the [air]port before dawn to await [Kar]pis.

Meanwhile, the fifteen-passenger [air]liner winged northward through [the] night, refueling in St. Louis [at]midnight and pausing at Kansas [City] from 2:13 to 5:36 A. M. to [a]void a storm.

Karpis Didn't Have Ghost Of A Chance!

Gunman Who Boasted He'd Never Be Taken Alive Surrenders Meekly to G-Men Led by Hoover

(Copyright, 1936, by Associated Press)
NEW ORLEANS, May 2.—Fed[er]al agents landed Alvin Karpis in [St.] Paul today to answer for the [...] murder and robbery that...

SUNDAY NIGHT EXTRA

PRICE TWO CENTS

Karpis Put Behind Bars In St. Paul

Notorious Outlaw Taken by Air From New Orleans to Scene of Two of His Kidnapings; Desperado Sullen, Cold and Weary After Hard Plane Trip

BY. ST. PAUL, May 2.—[AP]—[...]the outlaw, was brought back to St. Paul [...] on kidnaping charges.
[...] of justice agents who trapped the nation's [...] gunman in New Orleans late yesterday [...] in an overnight plane ride.
[Per]sonally by J. Edgar Hoover, department of [...] squad of picked agents, Karpis was landed [...] less than 12 hours after he was heavily-armed [...] ed out of New Orleans last night.

Wore Thin Summer Clothing

The desperado, wearing thin summer apparel in a tem[...]perature not above freezing, was hustled from the big

Giant German Dirigible En Route to Lakehurst

51 Passengers on Ship Ex[pe]cted to Reach U. S.

of 150 pictures one morning and told me to shuffle them into two piles, one of people I knew and the other of people I didn't know. I made three piles instead of two. I put some of the people I didn't know in one, a few people who were well-known friends of mine in another, and all of the others, which made up the majority of the pictures, in a third pile.

"What's this big pile in the middle?" McKee asked.

"There are some people I know in that pile," I said, "and some people I don't know, and I'll leave it to you guys to figure out who's who."

A big husky guy came into the room. He was an agent from somewhere outside St. Paul, and he was full of boasts. He told me that his father was a United States Senator and he told me that he was tough.

"I broke two telephone books on Doc Barker's head and back," he said. "I was so stiff and sore after I got through with him that I could hardly raise my arms over my head. Now, you wouldn't want me to go through the same thing with you, would you?"

I didn't answer. And I was relieved that the big guy never did have a crack at me. He could have snapped me in two.

McKee was the worst of all the agents. He was another boaster, and he kept telling me about the guys he'd put in prison. He got a big bang out of telling stories about innocent guys he'd helped to convict. He talked about a few guys I knew, robbers who were in jail for jobs I'd actually pulled. He thought that was funny.

I got in one dig at him. He told me about the night in Chicago in the fall of 1934 when he and some other agents could have killed Doc Barker.

"We were trailing Doc down Seventy-ninth Street in front of Sears Roebuck," McKee told me, "and we watched him pick up Earl Christman's wife. We could have killed him right on the spot if we'd wanted to. But we saved him. We wanted to set him up for a capture later on."

"I'll tell you something, McKee," I said. "You couldn't have done a thing. Freddie Barker and I were in a car right behind yours. We had a couple of machine guns trained on your Ford coupe."

Clinton Stein, the head of the St. Paul FBI office, interrupted me.

"What would you have done if McKee had tried to take Barker?" he asked.

"We would have cut him down."

McKee was sore as hell.

Later, he and some other agents pulled a dirty trick on me. They told me that they had Harry Campbell staked out in Ohio. They said they were just waiting to move in on him. But first, they said, they were going to tell the papers that they had broken me down and that I had given away Harry's hideout. I knew what that meant. It meant that if I went to prison, I'd be known among the inmates as a guy who had put his finger on a friend.

It was obvious to me that the agents were getting desperate. The days were going by and they had nothing to report to Hoover, nothing that did them any good. They concentrated most of their questions in the third and fourth days on the Hamm case. They wanted details on Jack Peifer's fix at St. Paul police headquarters. They brought the Bremer kidnapping into the questioning. They wanted to know how we'd managed to find out in advance each plan that the cops and the FBI had come up with for our capture. I wouldn't tell them anything, and their frustration just deepened.

The questioning ran on hour after hour. I was groggy and exhausted. Then, all of a sudden, around three o'clock one morning, the mood in the room changed. Telephones were ringing. Agents were scurrying in and out. And one of them brought me in a cot. The St. Paul chief, Stein, took some keys out of the desk and unlocked my shackles, and I sat on the cot.

"You're going before a commissioner in the morning," one agent told me, "and Mr. Hoover wants us to clean you up."

"What's the date?" I asked Stein.

"May sixth."

A couple of agents led me down the hall to the wash-room. They gave me more time than they'd allowed me before. I soaked my face in hot water, then in cold, and when the agents took me back to the cot, there were sweet buns waiting for me. And some coffee.

I sat on the cot, not sleeping, just slumped and staring, all through the morning and into the afternoon. At 3 P.M., Stein walked into the room and said it was time to go. I looked around the room.

"Is this what you want?" Stein asked.

He was holding my straw hat. It was in better shape than my shirt and pants after all those days chained to the radiator.

"Let's go," somebody said, and we walked down the halls, through some corridors, and into a commissioner's office. The building was jammed with people—photographers, reporters, office workers, curious people—and we had to push and shove through the whole route.

It was crowded in the court clerk's office, too, but I could hear every word he said. He read out four counts against me, two relating to the Hamm kidnapping, two to the Bremer kidnapping. Then he set bail—$100,000 on each of the four counts, $400,000 in all.

The deputy court clerk paused and looked up at me.

"And another hundred thousand on general principles," he said. "Do you care to make this bond today?"

"Well, hardly," I answered, and the line appeared in all the newspapers that night. So did the amount of the bail, $500,000, the highest bail ever charged against a criminal in United States history up to that date.

I thought I'd get a little peace when I left the clerk's

office. I expected to be turned over to the U.S. marshal's office. But I wasn't so lucky. I discovered that the FBI had taken over a section of the St. Paul jail just for me. The feds were my personal jailers. For the entire time I waited in the jail, at least one agent stood guard over me. The FBI men came in shifts, twenty-four hours a day. I was never alone. The sheriff and his men at the jail weren't allowed near me. An agent even cleaned out my cell each day.

Worst of all, the FBI sat within earshot of any conversations I had with my lawyers. I couldn't have a private consultation. The feds listened to everything. My first lawyer didn't really have anything to say to me that was worth anything. He told me flatly that my case was hopeless and that the cops were warning people not to help me. I fired him and took on another lawyer. He wasn't much better. He was intimidated by the FBI agents standing around my cell, and his main concern seemed to be that I wouldn't cause anyone any trouble.

I was taken before a judge for arraignment and, when all the charges were read out to me, I pleaded not guilty. I intended to stick to my plea, no matter what my lawyer wanted, no matter what the FBI demanded. The agents were after me constantly to appear before a grand jury and spill everything I knew about corruption in St. Paul, about the way Jack Peifer was able to bribe politicians and police officers. The U.S. District Attorney came to me and promised that if I pleaded guilty on the four counts, he'd get me a prison sentence, not death, and that the sentence would be of such a length that I would eventually get out and not die inside a penitentiary.

I listened to them all. I heard all the stories about the campaign the press was carrying on against me. I heard how I was the dreaded Public Enemy Number One as far as all the people on the outside were concerned. I heard that Hoover had brainwashed and threatened everyone con-

nected with my case. I heard that I didn't stand a chance.
No one could help me, it seemed. The only faint hope that
came to me from the outside was a present from old Chuck
Fitzgerald, who was also waiting trial in the Hamm kidnapping. Fitzgerald sent me some religious pamphlets. It was
a generous thought, but I didn't think the pamphlets would
help much in my defense.

When my trial was finally called a few weeks later, I still
hadn't made up my mind what I was going to do. I knew I
didn't have much of a defense or alibi, and I knew that my
lawyer was hardly in a class with Clarence Darrow. I walked
into the courtroom on the first day of trial, and I sat down
handcuffed to a marshal. I felt exhausted. I was discouraged.
I knew that I'd had it and, acting almost by impulse, I called
over my lawyer.

"I'm going to plead guilty."

"That's a good move," he said. He was happy to get out
from under the responsibility. "We wouldn't have had a
chance in this atmosphere."

My lawyer spoke to the district attorney, and everyone
was all smiles. It was agreed that the court would go ahead
only on one count of the Hamm charges. Then the judge
arrived and watched me stand up and say "guilty" after the
charge was read out. He ordered me taken back to the cells.
He wasn't interested in why I had changed my plea so suddenly.

Two weeks later, I walked back into the courtroom. It was
time for sentencing. I was expecting to hear the judge give
me a term of years, a sentence that would permit me to apply
for parole after a certain period. I was wrong.

He gave me life.

And the next day I took a train for Leavenworth, Kansas.
The FBI went with me. The agents still wouldn't trust me
to anyone. Not until I disappeared behind bars for my sentence of life in prison.

EPILOGUE

Freddie Barker was dead and so was Ma. FBI bullets had killed them. Frank Nash and John Dillinger were dead. So were Baby Face Nelson, Pretty Boy Floyd, Tommy Carroll, Homer Van Meter, John Hamilton, Earl Christman, and Bonnie Parker and Clyde Barrow. The cops had gunned them down. But they didn't all die fighting the police. Guys like Shotgun George Zeigler and Vern Miller and Gus Winkler were taken care of by the underworld. Elmer Higgins was finished off by a fast-draw druggist. And talkative characters like Doc Moran and Arthur Dunlop wound up as corpses because they became personal targets.

A lot of people whose paths crossed mine during my five-year crime spree were dead. And of the rest, most wound up in prison. Doc Barker, for instance. He went to Alcatraz for life for the Bremer kidnapping. Jack Peifer got a term of years for the Hamm kidnapping, then promptly committed suicide. Our old veteran Chuck Fitzgerald and Bartholmey, the Bensenville postmaster, also went to prison for the Hamm caper. Lawrence Devol got life for killing a cop in one of the Minneapolis bank jobs. Harry Campbell, Sam Coker, and Freddie Hunter all went to prison. And Dolores went to jail, too.

As for me, I entered Alcatraz on August 7, 1936. I was to spend more than twenty-five years on the Rock. No other inmate had ever spent that much time there. In 1962, I was transferred to the federal penitentiary on McNeil Island in Puget Sound, near Tacoma, Washington. There I stayed until

January, 1969, when I was paroled and deported to my native Canada.

In a way, my capture in New Orleans marked the end of an era. I was the last of the big-name public enemies of Depression-day America. I was the man J. Edgar Hoover wanted more than anybody.

Hoover should have been satisfied that I was in custody. But he wasn't content just to arrest me. He wanted to nail everybody who had ever befriended me. Conspiracy to harbor Alvin Karpis became a very serious matter. The Angus brothers, Ted and Burt, of Toledo, Ohio, found that out. So did Joe Roscoe, Edith Barry, Jim McGraw and a guy named Greenie who owned a fleet of taxicabs in Toledo. The FBI hounded them. Then the agents moved on to Cleveland where they went after Art Heberandt and Tony Amerback of the Harvard Club.

But it's the story of Grace Goldstein and the three Hot Springs, Arkansas, police officers that stands out. It really showed up the shoddy operations of Hoover and the high echelon of the FBI before and after my arrest. And I challenge Hoover to deny the accuracy of any part of the story.

It started for me one night in the St. Paul, Minnesota, jail after my interrogation. An agent assigned to watch me during the evening hours arrived with a briefcase which, he said, contained my file. He was pretty disillusioned with the way the FBI had handled my case and didn't mind me knowing how he felt.

"Karpis," he said, "let me read a little something out of your file."

Well, that *little something* was pretty interesting. The information that had led to my whereabouts in New Orleans had been obtained by agents of the Little Rock, Arkansas, office from a subject known only as Informant A. The identity of the informant was to be kept a top secret. It was not to be made known even to other agents.

Alvin Karpis as he Appears Today
FRANK PRAZAK, WEEKEND MAGAZINE

"A lot of people were dead. And most wound up in prison. Bartholmey, the Bensenville postmaster, also went to prison for the Hamm caper." — UPI

The fed who was telling me this smiled as he said, "Informant A can only be Grace Goldstein."

The news surprised me, but I couldn't work up any animosity for Grace. They had probably given her a bad time. Very few men could stand the pressure when the heat was on. So how could I expect a woman to go through it? Anyway, I didn't say anything. I listened and he went into a tirade about the FBI's top brass. He complained about the tactics they used trying to get me to put others in jail and then he went on about my arrest.

"They claim it was strictly an FBI production," he said. "But we know better."

The story had all kinds of twists and it would be a couple of years before I'd be able to put the pieces together. But it went back to the arrest of Frank Nash in Hot Springs. They took Nash to Kansas City by train, and two guys were waiting to rescue him at the railroad station. Well, several people were killed in the battle that broke out at the depot and the U.S. government immediately alleged that three of Hot Springs' top policemen had tipped the underworld off to the exact time of arrival of Nash's train. The cops named were chief of police Joe Wakelin, chief of detectives Herbert (Dutch) Akers, and the force's fingerprint expert, a lieutenant named Cecil Brock.

The cops beat the rap and this upset the FBI. In fact, Hoover and some of his agents smoldered for some time over this. Then they decided to get Grace Goldstein to help frame the three cops. If they could pressure her into testifying for the government, the case was in the bag. She refused, though, and the feds gave her a pass for a couple of years. Finally, they succeeded in building a case against the cops and they indicted her along with them. All four went to prison on charges of harboring me. In Grace's case, it happened to be true. She *had* harbored me. But the cops were entirely innocent.

I did a little smoldering myself in Alcatraz. About the way they acted with Grace Goldstein and how they used me and Ma Barker to make big heroes of themselves. The FBI had never been among my favorite people, but I came to despise their methods after my arrest and interrogation. It's kind of understating it when I say I resented the way Hoover and his men treated me in that situation. I couldn't call a lawyer. I was held incommunicado for days. I was subjected to third-degree tactics. In short, I was denied every civil right.

It's an old practice of the FBI to dress up the truth with lies that make them look more clever and powerful than they really are. The most glaring example of their deceitful sense of public relations, though, came after my New Orleans capture. The myth soon spread, helped by the FBI's own testimony, that Hoover himself led the arresting agents.

The official version of what happened that day in New Orleans is in a book written by Don Whitehead called *The FBI Story*. The facts were taken from FBI files. And, just to make the account as official as possible, Hoover wrote a foreword to the book. The story is that I was sitting in the front seat of the car when Hoover and his agents approached. I made a move for a rifle lying on the back seat. Hoover jerked open the door on the driver's side and grabbed me. At the same time, an agent named Connelly dove into the car from the passenger's side and also grabbed me. The two then hustled me away from my rifle.

Over the years in prison, a lot of people questioned me about my arrest. U.S. Attorney Generals, Senators, Congressmen, and prison officials visited me and every last one of them asked the same question: Did Hoover really arrest me personally? My only reply to them was, "Why don't you ask Mr. Hoover?"

Well, the time has come to set the record straight:

The FBI story of my arrest is totally false. Just as false

as the one that Hoover put out in 1935 to the effect that I had sent him a note threatening to kill him.

How could Connelly have dived in through the passenger side of the car when my friend Freddie Hunter was sitting beside me? He surely would have blocked Connelly's way.

And the rifle in the back seat. What rifle? What back seat? We were in a 1936 Plymouth coupe that had no back seat. We had two rifles, but they were wrapped in a blanket to prevent damage to the sights, and they were locked away in the luggage compartment.

The most obvious flaw in the FBI story, though, lies in Hoover's own character. He didn't lead the attack on me. He hid until I was safely covered by many guns. He waited until he was told the coast was clear. Then he came out to reap the glory.

The story of Hoover the Hero is false.

Over the many years I spent in prison—I was eligible for parole after fifteen years but they kept me in for thirty-three— it grated on me that Americans had been gulled into cheering Hoover as one of the country's great men on the basis of his version of my arrest. That May day in 1936, I made Hoover's reputation as a fearless lawman. It's a reputation he doesn't deserve.

I have nothing but contempt for J. Edgar Hoover.

For the rest, there are no apologies, no regrets, no sorrows, and no animosity. What happened happened.